UNDETERRED

The Success Equation of Women of Black and Asian Heritage

CLAUDIA CRAWLEY

DEDICATION

For Aunt Dor, my second mom and my role model. A courageous woman: a family pioneer who walked that lonely path taken by young, smart, ambitious black women of the Windrush generation. The odds may have been stacked against her, but she remained undeterred and prospered.

FOREWORD

For the decade that I have known Claudia Crawley, she has been a tireless advocate for change in the lives of women. Whether in her role as an executive coach, speaker, or trainer, or the many philanthropic ways in which she serves, she ensures that the excluded voice is represented in every room in which she is present. Her passion and commitment are clear, and the clarity and directness of her message leaves no doubt.

With Claudia's robust credentials and extensive experience, I have had the pleasure of inviting her to be a panellist at numerous diversity and inclusion events. Every time I leave a conversation with Claudia, I have additional insight and am challenged, and I am better for it.

Alongside her participation in the fight for gender equality is her long-term involvement in anti-racist activism. Clearly, it is in her blood to give a voice to those who have experienced oppression, which makes her the ideal person to write this book.

So, what can you expect from this book? Well just like any conversation with Claudia, it will challenge your ideas and generate new insights. It will introduce you to the Success Equation comprising the elements shared by these women of colour striving to achieve.

Claudia's unique voice and the stories of struggle, tenacity and accomplishments that are shared illuminate the intersection of identity that women of colour in the UK experience. Claudia's well-honed journalistic skills developed through her Page 1 Women series enhance the stories within this book.

If you are a woman of colour, you will find yourself identifying with at least one of these Page 1 Women, nodding your head in agreement to their lived experiences or things you know, but that are often unsaid, or that you hadn't acknowledged before.

However, this book does not just take what is said at face value but enquires and digs deeper, and even codifies the lessons to make the Success Equation, which makes it memorable—something Claudia is exceptional at. You'll love the tips and lessons in every chapter.

If you are not a woman of colour, don't worry—this book is for you, too. You may be in the process of trying to educate yourself in the complex world of race and gender; this can be challenging, especially if you don't want to burden those who may have experienced discrimination and bias in the past with your education. This book will help. It will provide a window into the personal and professional lives of women of colour and how you can be a true ally to them.

As an award-winning coach who has been working in the field of gender and racial equality for the past twenty years, I know that we still have a long way to go to achieve gender parity, and systemic racism still sadly exists in society. But with the help of Claudia's motivating and empowering words, the lessons from the women of colour shared within this book, and the Success Equation, I believe we can accelerate change and, indeed, be undeterred!

Jenny Garrett OBE
Award-Winning Executive Coach,
Leadership Trainer and founder of the
Diverse Executive Coach Directory

ACKNOWLEDGEMENTS

Many thanks go to Denise Roberts, from The Editor's Chair, my book coach, and skilful editor. Thanks for nudging, guiding, and helping me reach the finishing line.

Donal Carroll, my partner who never tired of reading, re-reading and sharing your expertise with the written word.

Meta Groselj, my dear friend and accountability buddy who checked on me and kept me to task.

Rupinder Dehal, Carol Stewart, Judith Chambers-Thomas; Aliyah Dunbar-Hussain; Yasmin Sheikh, my readers who gave their time and provided constructive feedback.

Johnson Purple, graphic designer and my book illustrator.

Jen Heil, for creating my social media posts and ensuring I got word of the book out to the digital world.

And most of all, to all my Undeterred Page 1 Women, without whom there would be no book.

TABLE OF CONTENTS

CHAPTER 1

Why the Book?

'Sometimes, I feel discriminated against, but it does not make me angry. It merely astonishes me. How can anyone deny themselves the pleasure of my company? It's beyond me.'

— Zora Neale Hurston

One ordinary morning of another ordinary working day, I was scrolling through my social media feed when I noticed something. The detail escapes me, but I remember the indignation I felt. The post itself seemed innocuous, but the hatred, vile stereotyping and cruel insinuations it attracted, mainly from white women, were overwhelming. What exactly had this woman done to deserve this kind of reaction, I wondered. How had the name 'Megan Markle' become so swiftly synonymous with loathing?

The idea of *'Undeterred'* emerged through a combination of this indignation at the way black women are treated by the UK tabloid press and social media trolls, and my longstanding mission to shine a light on successful women who are working hard, often quietly, behind the scenes and worthy of the front-page status. Many of these women face challenges similar to Meghan Markle: the gender and racial micro-aggressions, the aggressive black woman trope, double standards, and other discrimination reinforced by the mainstream tabloids and social media minus the obvious privileges she enjoys.

I became preoccupied with this relentless Meghan-bashing. Then one morning, during my meditation routine, the brainchild of this book popped into my head. It quickly became my big goal for 2021.

I wondered how Meghan Markle was dealing with the persistent demonisation of her character. I pondered how she would have responded if she, like me, had no access to state power, privilege, and prosperity. Who would she turn to for support? What would be her strategies? What would keep her going? How would her story pan out?

The Book

I wanted this book to emphasise:

- The everyday challenges faced by a group of women our society seldom heeds, especially black British and Asian British working women, for whom the intersection of race and gender makes their lived experiences inarguably different from those of white women. Whilst some people would prefer to ignore that uncomfortable fact, we encounter obstacles that white women don't due to our skin colour.
- The actions these women take to overcome those challenges.
- The ingredients of their success.
- What other black and Asian British women could learn from their experiences given that books tackling such issues are scarce in the UK, though becoming less so.
- The value and success of my chosen group of women, who obviously struggle at times with heavy knocks to their confidence but may not be aware of their impact. Yet, they all contribute in their own way towards making the world a better place.

My Page 1 Women

My choice of women has, of course, been deliberate. Some are long-standing members of my personal and professional networks. Others were added more recently as I navigated life as a business owner, joined business development groups, such as Andy Harrington's Professional Speakers Academy, and grew as a feminist. My aim to showcase extraordinary ordinary women has honed my antenna for identifying such people. Yes, they are successful, but they aren't the usual suspects: the celebrities or the millionaires with the perfect hair, make-up, or size nought bodies we are supposed to strive for. These are regular women, relatable women, ambitious women with a clear vision of where they want to go. Purposeful women who have made or are making their indelible mark in the world. These women have devised strategies that help them flourish despite the challenges they face. They are women others can look up to and say, 'If she can do it, so can I.' These are my Page 1 Women.

The idea for the Page 1 Woman originated a while back, in protest against the 'Page Three Girls'; those glamour models once displayed topless on page three of the British tabloid newspaper, *The Sun*. Whilst these women were celebrated for the sizes of their breasts and their youthful good looks, my Page 1 Women would be celebrated for their intellect and contribution to the world without even an iota of regard to their physical appearance.

The black and Asian Page 1 Women interviewed in this book are a rich mix of age and experience. They come from a variety of backgrounds—some born in the UK, others abroad—who have made this country their home. They operate in a variety of industries and may have found success in employment, in their own business, or in political or social causes that stir their passions.

Alongside what they have achieved, what these women have strikingly in common is that they are self-leaders: 'A comprehensive self-influence perspective that concerns leading oneself toward performance of naturally motivating tasks as well as managing oneself to do work that must be done but is not naturally motivating.'[1] Or, in Peter Drucker's phrase, 'To self-lead is to serve as chief, captain, or CEO of one's own life.'[2] It involves independence, setting one's own targets, making one's own decisions, and developing oneself to flourish and endure in an uncertain, unpredictable and complex world. It is a prerequisite for leading others effectively. These women are leaders.

Leadership

There is no unifying perspective or agreed definition of leadership. However, one I find useful is 'a process of social influence, which

---

1   Charles Manz, 1986.
2   Peter Drucker, 2010.

maximises the efforts of others, towards the achievement of a goal.'[3] This gives it direction and purpose. It is further broadened by saying leadership:

- 'Stems from social influence, not authority or power';
- Influences others, implying they don't need to be 'direct reports';
- Is not dependent on personality traits, attributes, or even a title; 'There are many styles, many paths, to effective leadership'; and
- Includes a goal rather than influence without an intended outcome.[4]

This definition appeals to me for three reasons:

1. It challenges the traditional idea of boss-man leadership.

2. It includes democratised leadership at its heart; we can all be leaders when we have the courage and the will to be so. We don't have to be the white boss-man.

3. It involves maximising the efforts of other people towards a particular goal, whether it's an idea, an action or a policy. In other words, we're enabling others to get engaged, encouraging and perhaps rewarding them in their efforts to achieve an identified aim.

How many people do you know who lead, not because they are designated leaders, but because they are influential and can get the best out of people? A young woman who springs to mind for me is Greta Thunberg. Her actions, knowledge, and clear arguments have engaged children and young people across the globe in the fight against the destruction of the planet. My Page 1 Women are leaders who toll in line with this definition, whether they are heading an organisation or a movement or whether they are employees.

Rather than impose this definition on my Page 1 Women during their interviews, I encouraged them to self-define. My aim was to discover through whatever definition they offered whether they see themselves as leaders. These women may be in leadership positions

3   Kevin Kruse, 'What is Leadership?' Forbes 9 April 2013.
4   Kevin Kruse, 'What is Leadership?' Forbes 9 April 2013.

such as senior management or a CEO. They may have leadership experiences, perhaps learned through role modelling teachers or parents and enacting that learning, or developed through their roles as influential big sisters, amongst their peers in the playground, or as a school head girl, for example. And there is the contradiction: most of them did not consider themselves leaders until prompted by my question.

But this is in no way an uncommon phenomenon. My experience as an executive coach specialising in working with women has revealed that the conventional expectation of men as leaders and women as followers is carved in the minds of many women. The mainstream issue that white men are leaders and black women shouldn't even be there hangs thickly in the air, noticed but unsaid.

These women are definitely self-leaders, and leaders with social influence prepared to share their experiences, of navigating workplace challenges due to gender and skin colour alongside their stories of success. They are leaders who also wish to inspire another generation of regular black and Asian women. They are relatable role models who may not consciously see themselves as such, and may even fight against being labelled as such, but role models they are. Interestingly, there were other black and Asian women I approached to be part of the book—women who worked in the law profession or male-dominated industries such as construction and engineering. Much to my disappointment, but understandably, they declined because they felt they would be putting their reputation and livelihoods at risk should they dare to speak out about their experience of racism and sexism in their respective fields. What does this say about 21st century Britain, when black and Asian women are afraid to speak out about inequality and micro-aggressions at work?

My Method

In getting acquainted with these women and unpacking their experiences, they were interviewed using the same set of questions. Although some women found the topics of race and gender more difficult than others, certain themes emerged.

Themes:

1. **These women are 'difficult':** A term used by men about gutsy, badass women who aren't easily influenced and controlled by men. It's also used by those white people who find it hard to control trouble-making black and brown women who ask questions. These Page 1 Women aren't inherently problematic, but they are considered so by people who label women like them 'difficult'. They are women who have grappled with the status quo in order to engage with the systemic challenges of racism and sexism. They are black women who refused to sit back and accept misogynoir, and Asian women and Muslim women who have defied the prevailing stereotypes that often restrict their potential. They are women who have found a way through—their own way, the one that worked for them at the time. These are hang-in-there women who weren't prepared to give up on their ambitions.

2. **Different names, similar experiences:** There is a generational influence on identity names. An older Asian woman sees herself as black, a reflection of the 1980s and 90s when 'black' was used as a political term to denote all those who experienced racism. Younger women tend to say 'women of colour' or Asian. So, throughout the book, you'll find a variety of terms: black, Asian, women of colour, and, one I'm particularly fond of, global majority communities.

3. **Varying perspectives:** Some of these women did not perceive racism or sexism at the time. This could be for a variety of reasons: an unconscious coping strategy perhaps; accepting their experiences as just another fact of life rather than a phenomenon with a label; or perhaps blaming themselves, rather than the system—typical of women when their self-esteem is low or they are gaslighted. Whichever the case, their individual coping strategy worked for them. With time to grow and reflect, and with that wonderful thing called hindsight, they are now able to acknowledge what was going on. This could be a reflection of the learning journey towards

racial and gender clarity that some of us from global majority communities often have to make. It's a journey from seeing racism as non-existent or something that happens to other people to recognising that this is a common and very real-life experience.

4. **Planned disregarding**: Some women consciously chose to ignore issues around race and gender which, for them, was a safer and easier option. It may have smacked of tolerance, of failing to support other black and Asian women, but it worked for them. One woman saw the issues for her as being more about poverty and money rather than race and gender. These were the main challenges in her cultural community and her childhood home. Could it be that these were convenient ways for the community to cover up classism and sexism?

5. **Getting support**: As leaders, whether appointed or assumed, where did they get their support? Not from other black and brown women, in some cases, because there weren't any there. Such women chose white women colleagues or managers they admired as their supporters. And, although direct experience of racism was missing from the frames of reference of these supporters, these Page 1 Women took what was available and found what worked for them. Other women relied on close family members or networks of friends. Regardless of where their support came from, sharing their challenges with trusted fans and being applauded for their achievements played an essential role in their journey.

6. **Mental health**: When racism and sexism chip away at one's self-esteem and sense of self, there is an inevitable impact on one's mental health. Some of the women spoke of having to be strategic about their battles as a way of managing the regular assault on their dignity. As fighting every micro-aggression and injustice is unsustainable, they had to decide which to fight and which to abandon, which would have a bigger impact, and which could be tackled another time. It's an exhausting and time-guzzling experience that can easily

eat into other priorities such as your relationships so that loved ones get the worst rather than the best of you.

Choosing to withdraw when feeling weighed down is not about quitting but protecting one's well-being and loved ones. It's about preserving one's energy, guarding one's time, and ensuring that we live to fight another day.

Popular opinion says that we always 'play the race card'. If we did, we would collapse with burnout. So when you see successful women from global majority communities and you think, 'Great, she's made it,' just ask yourself, 'What price has she paid to get there?'

Finding the Success Equation

Despite their diversity in terms of class, age, occupations, and ethnicity, there is a common denominator that unites my Page 1 Women, which has enabled them to thrive. It takes the form of a group of elements that these women embody, and I have constructed them into an equation for success: $D + R^2 + P$, or Determination + Resilience & Resistance + Purpose.

Constructing the Equation

In identifying the success equation, the question I asked was, 'Do these women have something that other go-getters lack? And if so, what is it?' Common elements of success for any go-getter regardless of background seem to be determination, resilience and purpose. But what makes the equation different for my Page 1 Women is that, from my observations, they possess the following:

1. Determination, resilience and purpose aplenty, which emphasises the saying 'black people need to work twice as hard to get half as far'.

2. An additional element in the equation: resistance. Because they are not white, these women face additional and continual oppression. Just being who they are and living their regular lives, they attract additional pressures that the intersection of race and gender brings; pressures that do not exist on the shelves of white achievers. They were forced to find a

way to deal with it. And resistance was and is their way. For black and Asian women, resistance is about crossing those additional rivers.

These two differences create a success equation for black and Asian women.

$D+R^2+P$—Determination + Resilience & Resistance + Purpose. These four elements are interconnected, interdependent with fluid boundaries. All are necessary to be effective.

Unpacking the Equation

Determination: My Page 1 Women have grit, tenacity in abundance, and are resolute. They have dazzling determination. Determination was built and refined through the following examples:
- Encountering racist behaviour from colleagues, and managers failed to support them;
- White male team members refused to accept their management authority;
- Complaints of racist behaviour in the company were not taken seriously or were ignored; and/or
- Their knowledge, skills, and credibility as managers were questioned.

So how did they respond? They chose to focus and persevere and became unstoppable.

Resilience: This is the chamber of strength that my Page 1 Women access when in need. Aburn et al[5] saw resilience as being about overcoming adversity and thriving, maintaining mental stability, and bounce-back-ability from hardship. In other words, resilience is the psychological trampoline. Examples that engaged their need for resilience go from the everyday to the more extreme. For example:

---

5 Aburn, G., Gott, M., & Hoare, K. (2016). What is resilience? An integrative review of the empirical literature. Journal of Advanced Nursing, 72, 980–1000.

- Accused of being a quota rather than employed on merit, one woman bided her time to find the best way to challenge it;
- Denied development opportunities, another created alternative opportunities for herself;
- After surviving domestic abuse, another used her experiences to create a service that benefited others; and
- Faced with threats of violence, another managed her emotions and didn't allow these threats to faze her as she pursued her goals.

Resilience is in the DNA of black and Asian people due, in my view, to the legacy of unaddressed colonial attitudes. Here's an example: *It often feels that, as a woman, as black women, we are only celebrated, loved, and applauded for our resilience. Our ability to keep going and survive in systems that oppress us day in and day out can often feel like the only way others see us as human or see us as worthy of praise.*[6] This kind of response to resilience is an oblique form of racism; the stereotype of the strong black woman who is not allowed to be vulnerable and get support. Yet, at the same time, we know that black and Asian women need to be resilient. As Charlene White, journalist and newsreader, once said, 'I wouldn't be where I am today without resilience.'

Resistance: Resistance is about confronting oppressive behaviour, making your stand, and always having one more ploy than your antagonist.

So how did these Page 1 Women resist?

- Refusing to collude with excluding behaviour;
- Quitting oppressive workplaces to set up their own business;
- Leading a political party committed to equality; and
- Getting involved in collective action by campaigning for an equality cause.

These women have been true to the spirit of this quote by Dr. Martin Luther King: 'We must learn that passively to accept

---

6 Black Ballad, 23.5.21 Toby Oredein.

an unjust system is to cooperate with that system, and thereby to become a participant in its evil.'

Purpose: Purpose, in this context, refers to a strategic aim or intention that contributes something to change the world. It is the most powerful element within the success equation, and my Page 1 Women have it in abundance.

Their purposes included:
- Making affordable housing accessible in London;
- Gender equality;
- Supporting youngsters facing mental health issues; and,
- Increasing the value of the Human Resources function in organisations.

Their purpose provided fuel and focused their commitment. It became the source of their staying power. Purpose creates transforming energy so that when these women were professionally ignored, or their sense of self came under attack, it brought hope, optimism, and courage. Through their purpose, each woman has made a difference in the world. So their purpose is much bigger than them; it is the cornerstone of the success equation.

The need for the success equation

The road to success, however you wish to define it, is testing yet a fulfilling adrenaline booster. What's clear is that, for these black and Asian women, a certain formula worked. $D + R^2 + P$ is a formula that brings together the most powerful ingredients for success for these women. This is the equation that enabled their success against a backdrop of stereotyping, regular micro-aggressions, marginalisation, misogyny, and race hatred. This book is a celebration and a story of the spirit of black and Asian women who have made their mark. Far from rolling over and passively tolerating unfairness and discrimination, these Page 1 Women have faced the challenges and discovered their particular way to hit back.

They are also ordinary folk

'It is important to focus on ordinary folk. If you believe it is only amazing people who can do great things, you do not realise you can do it, too. The reason people teach the great man theory is to immobilise you, then they've got you.'[7]

As you read on, I hope you will be as inspired by the stories of my Page 1 Women as I was in interviewing them.

---

7 Judy Richardson, Civil Rights Activist.

CHAPTER 2

Sharda: The Social Worker

What is it about social workers that attract bad press? Previous research indicates that the social work profession, particularly its social workers, are often criticised and misrepresented by the UK press. Historically vilified by tabloid newspapers like[8] *The Daily Mail* and *The Sun* for unfathomable reasons and labelled 'do-gooders' and interfering by parents, you would be forgiven for thinking that child protection social workers were totally inept. And yet, pandemic or not, social workers safeguard society's most vulnerable. All this exists against a backdrop of complex cases, scarce resources, and ever-increasing workloads. Without them, society would not function efficiently. But here's the good news: A recent survey indicated a favourable shift in the British public's perception of social workers.[9] Clearly, they are doing something very right.

It's a well-known fact that social work is a challenging profession. With demanding cases involving the most vulnerable, ever-increasing workloads and diminishing resources, high-stress levels come with the territory. So I reckon that it takes a special type of person to choose social work as a profession. People who are not in it for the money. People who are committed to the role. People who actually care.

For example, here is my Page 1 Woman, Sharda Parthasarathi. A social worker for 30-odd years, her journey into the profession started when she was still a teenager. Ridiculed by the career adviser for her choice of profession, Sharda didn't care. She went for it anyway. Determination, ambition, courage, and sheer staying power

---

8   Ayre, 2001; Reid & Misener, 2001; Warner, 2014; Hughes & Houston, 2019.
9   'Perceptions of Social Work' Social Work England, May 2020.

enabled her to make a great success of it. Seldom could a career adviser have got it so badly wrong.

But it hasn't all been plain sailing. As one of very few Asian social workers in the North of England, Sharda found the work utterly rewarding and yet difficult. In those early days, social work managers knew little about the different Asian cultures, so that when Sharda ran into challenging situations with clients who shared aspects of her culture, support was limited. These were often the most demanding cases for an Asian social worker perceived by her community as being in cahoots with a hostile system.

So, how did Sharda navigate the two worlds? How did she do so successfully? Let's find out.

THE INTERVIEW

Claudia: Sharda, what do you do for a living?

Sharda: I'm a registered social worker and an independent social work consultant. I currently chair fostering panels. I'm also a consultant for a number of fostering companies, which have included the positions of non-executive director and auditor.

In addition, I've recently been a lead reviewer of a serious case review.[10] So, my role these days is very much about the quality-assuring practice.

My work is mainly around looked-after children, children who, for reasons such as neglect or abuse, are unable to live at home. But I'm open to anybody approaching me with work around safeguarding children. I currently work with three local authorities and three independent fostering and adoption agencies.

Claudia: It's well-known that social work is a demanding profession. So, what got you into it?

Sharda: I started in social work as a volunteer at the age of about 15. I qualified as a social worker when I was only 22. So I've been a social worker all of my adult life. At the age of 15, I became a member of the local community centre. My mum was the treasurer, and one day I was grounded for bad behaviour. My dad was out, my sister had already left for university, and my mum had a meeting at the centre. Rather than leave me grounded at home alone, she made me go to the committee meeting with her. I sat quietly in the corner and took the minutes.

The chair of the committee, at that time, was the Mayor of Halifax. He was aware of me sucking my teeth and puffing and blowing as they talked about setting up a youth club. To this 15-year-old, they had no idea. The mayor said, 'I would be really interested in your input.' So I joined in. At the end of the meeting, I accepted his invitation to become a committee member. I helped set up the youth club and a community-based nursery. This was the early 1980s before young people's participation had developed. At 16, I was on the interview panel interviewing managers at the community centre.

10 An inquiry that is carried out when a child dies or is seriously harmed.

I also became a probation service volunteer advising and assisting two young people whose dads had just been given life sentences. I worked with a particular probation officer who liked my style and enthusiasm.

My parents first came to the UK from India in 1964, before I was born. Both were very well-educated and could speak, read, and write in English. They came to a community where there were lots of Indian and Pakistani people from less educated backgrounds and who were illiterate in English. When I was tiny, we always had weekend visitors with forms to fill in and advice to seek. And I thought that was what everybody's parents did. I grew up in an environment where helping people was what you did in order to belong to a community, and I was influenced into doing social work.

I knew it was social work that I wanted to do because, when I was 15, I read an article about child abuse, as it was called at the time. And I was devastated that there were children and young people who didn't have happy childhoods. I was moved beyond belief that I had such loving parents who gave me so much and made me who I am. I found it distressing that some children didn't have that same kind of parenting.

Now, interestingly, my sister and I went to a grammar school. The careers adviser laughed at me and said, 'Social work? What a ridiculous career!' It was when social workers weren't required to be qualified, so it wasn't seen as a meaningful academic career. But I didn't listen. I started my A levels at the grammar school, but psychology and sociology weren't on offer. So, I wasted my whole lower sixth doing maths, economics, and general studies, which I didn't enjoy. When I realised that it wasn't for me, I messed about and organised parties in the pub and got a very poor end-of-year results. So, I left and went to the local college and did psychology and sociology A levels, plus a health and social care course. It allowed me to do different social care placements, which helped me to realise that I wanted to work with young people. I then began to pursue it more seriously.

When I was 18, I got my first job in a residential unit. Later, I became a social work assistant and family aid alongside volunteering for the Probation Service. That helped me get sessional jobs with youth workers running groups for the youth offending team. And then, at 21, I went away to qualify as a social worker.

My first job as a qualified social worker was in a local authority social services department. I was there for 10 years and quite quickly got promoted to a senior practitioner, and then acted up to team manager. Then I worked with a well-known children's charity as a first and second-line manager responsible for services across West Yorkshire. Three years ago, I moved into my current role as a self-employed independent social work consultant.

Although my main role is to chair fostering panels, quality assurance is what interests me most and where I see my future. I want to work on safeguarding improvements, especially around black and disabled children.

In terms of my career, I was always at the sharp end of child protection work. I got my taste for fostering when my husband and I fostered an Asian young person who became a member of our family. Fostering her started as an accident because there were very few social workers of colour in that local authority at the time, and that was what she needed. Then it became a longer-term/forever placement.

That first-hand experience of fostering got me interested in doing what I'm doing now. I learned about the long-term issues of a foster child and the need for foster parents to understand cultural concerns fully. I saw how I could use this learning to help foster carers be better parents for looked-after children. So that's what drew me back into fostering.

Claudia: So you got into social work and rose up the ranks, but what were the essential steps that got you to where you are now?

Sharda: The essential steps would have to be around understanding my identity as an Indian woman. Bear in mind that my mum and dad were the only people in the extended family to come to the UK. So I never had extended family around me, but I understood its importance. My mum would make us write letters to my relatives regularly and stay connected with them.

My parents chose to live in a very white, Catholic-Irish community. We had lots of similarities in terms of being immigrants who experienced discrimination, but we weren't the same. My sister and I were the only two brown faces playing out.

In the 1970s, to have brown faces and to enjoy the richness of our culture and join in with everything else was a difficult endeavour. But my parents managed it well. So, we were part of the swim team, played the violin, went to Brownies and dance classes. It's partly because my mom was always very active, and we got it from her. She was a positive role model, very sporty, and worked full-time for as long as I can remember. She was a civil servant in the HMRC for 35 years. At that time, it was the most hated profession in the country. She would tell people she was a civil servant rather than a tax officer for all the obvious reasons. She was also the North England HMRC badminton champion three years on the trot. So I learned loyalty, dependability, and hard work.

My dad was the first feminist I knew before I knew the word 'feminism.' He grew up where they were proud of their boys. But he had two girls, and he was proud of them, celebrated them, and pushed them forward despite the bias towards boys. Have you ever heard of the phrase 'Pink Ladu'? In any South Asian community, boys are seen as superior to girls. And, traditionally, new parents of boys would buy hundreds of cheap yellow Indian sweets called Ladus and give them to friends and the community. Well, my dad flipped the whole thing on its head and distributed them regardless when I was born. At our big Indian weddings, my dad would put his hand behind my back as though encouraging me to step forward.

So, in terms of essential steps, it would be getting that balance right of being proud to be a woman and proud of my Indian heritage while living in a white community.

I was about five when I became aware of myself as an Indian girl. Whilst playing out on the streets, I was told, 'No, you can't join the boys playing football because you're a girl.' And I'd say, 'Well, watch me and then decide whether you want me to join in or not.'

I also realised that most of my friends' mothers didn't work, even my white friends. And I remember thinking, 'What's that about?' So, although I wanted my mum to be around more because she had a full-time job, what I didn't seem to appreciate was that she actually was—more than I realised. She was playing with us in the street, and she was often the best bowler and batter when we played cricket.

There were some struggles with my identity. For example, during adolescence, my parents became more protective in saying, 'As an Indian girl, you can't go out.' But I pushed boundaries and struggled with that identity. And when I was around 19, I went backpacking in India with a white friend for eight months. We stayed with family along the way. And I was drawn back to my Indian identity during that trip.

But I purposefully avoided using my identity during my career. When I first started in social work, I wanted to be recognised as a good social worker first and foremost, not as an Indian woman social worker. So I probably pushed my identity aside. I purposefully worked in a very deprived, all-white community where child protection cases came in every day; lots of single parents, poverty, or criminal activity.

When I first qualified, I knew that to achieve great things I'd have to put my hand up. So, when I'd been qualified for four years, I became a senior practitioner in a new child protection post despite people telling me I hadn't enough experience. I held the most complex cases and got myself informed by reading stuff like New Messages from Research, the Cleveland Inquiry into Sexual Abuse, and new legislation. I probably became a know-it-all. I worked really hard because I didn't want anybody to say that I'd been appointed as the token black woman brought in by special government funding to increase the numbers of minority ethnic workers. I wanted to be there for my skills, strengths, and experiences. I moved jobs to an area where there was a significant Pakistani/Bangladeshi community. I knew I had the skills, that I'd got the job on merit, and that there was something I could do specifically for this community.

Another essential step was about forming relationships with stakeholders, and here my identity helped. The social work practice I developed was relationship-based; in other words, forming positive relationships with the child and walking in their shoes; with the family (even if I had to take their at-risk child into care); with partnering agencies such as health visitors, schools, anybody involved with that family; and with my own organisation (i.e. a relationship with the policies, procedures and legislation). I believe you can only form good relationships and have conversations with integrity if you are clear about your identity and can share this openly and honestly.

Claudia: Social work is really full of complexities. So, what challenges did you face, and how did you overcome them?

Sharda: Social work is a challenging profession. If it was easy, then we wouldn't have so many Serious Case Reviews of children seriously harmed or even killed. It's complicated and never straightforward, particularly in child protection work. Decisions are always made on the balance of risk. No social worker wants to remove a child from a family, but they have to do that because of the balance of risk and ultimately safeguard that child.

In my current roles, I'm still often staggered by some of the language that foster carers use when caring for black children. Supervising social workers often fail to challenge such language, although they know it's unacceptable.

My biggest challenges were when I worked in child protection with families from my own South Asian community. And, as a senior practitioner, I had the most complex cases. For example, I was the social worker of a mum's unborn baby after an older child had been killed. Family members were manipulative, saying, 'Are you one of them, or are you one of us?' They referred to me as a 'coconut'—brown on the outside, white on the inside. It was more hurtful than being called a 'Paki' because people were saying that I was turning my back on my culture and identity. I didn't get much support from management because they felt they had insufficient knowledge about working with Asian families. They just left me to get on with it. But it was a complex case, so I needed supervision.

The manipulation included being offered gifts and demands that I call the grandparents 'auntie and uncle' as we do in my culture. The hardest bit wasn't the child protection work that I was good at, but the pull-on identity and my culture. But I kept my head down and focused on safeguarding the children there. My South Asian origin didn't help me to form relationships with that family, but it did give me an insight into inter-family dynamics within the culture. It also helped me make decisions about placing the baby when it was born and circumventing the manipulation.

Another big challenge was having to blow the whistle on a senior manager who'd committed serious offences. He'd been very supportive in my early career, so it was traumatic, particularly as it was shrouded in secrecy. The enquiry lasted several years and concluded with a prosecution. I ended up having to get counselling, which put things in perspective. And I remained true to my values, kept my head down, and carried on.

I didn't take any time off work for any of these challenges. I just continued to be a great social worker. But something had to cave in, and I wasn't good at home. I neglected my partner. But he was great—very supportive.

As a woman of colour, I always had defiance about me; standing with my shoulders back, fists clenched and saying 'Yeah!' It probably hindered me around those challenges because I was afraid to show any vulnerability. So, looking back, I could have managed that differently.

I've had challenges around managing staff. Social work is a predominantly white female profession, so I've managed mainly white women. When I worked in a multi-cultural northern city, I employed mainly Pakistani women to reflect the local community. As a senior manager and woman of colour, there were times when I became their mum when I shouldn't have. It's important to be a caring manager, but to get that balance right was sometimes tricky.

I could manage projects, services, and child protection work. But managing staff from my community was trickier. They would also ask, 'Are you one of them or one of us?' Well, the answer was, 'I'm both. I'm going to be empathic, sensitive, warm and caring, and ensure that you get the right support to do your job.'

Equally, when I joined this very white organisation with very few black managers, at my first management meeting, I volunteered to cover another manager's leave. My white colleagues started talking about me as if I wasn't there. One of the men said, 'I'm not happy about Sharda covering my patch because I don't think she's got enough child protection knowledge and experience.' I looked behind me whilst thinking, 'Doesn't he realise I'm still in the room?'

In fact, I'd just come from managing an Initial Response Team[11] in a local authority. So I probably had more hands-on child protection experience than most of them. But they made assumptions, probably because of my age (I was just 30) and my being a black woman. They may have assumed that my colour got me the post in a multi-cultural city. So it was a challenge having to always prove myself by constantly putting my hand up for additional pieces of work, which then impacted my ability to do the job. Throughout my career, I felt I always had to prove myself. I spread myself thinly, and it impacted my health and well-being.

And there were many benefits of being a manager of colour supervising staff of colour. For example, I remember supervising a Pakistani social work assistant. Within a few years of coming to Britain, she had gained her nursery nursing qualification and learned English. One of her cases was a vulnerable Pakistani family whom she supported in the mother tongue. In supervision, she'd try to talk about the case in English, but the issues and concerns got diluted in translation. She was quite instinctive and intuitive, so what you learned was not just the words and the translation but the feelings within her first language. As she struggled to find the right words, I allowed her to share in Urdu. Now, my knowledge of Urdu was limited, but I could understand all her words, and I picked up the tone, intonation, body language and learned so much more about the issues than I ever could have spoken in English. I formed a nurturing relationship with this woman and helped her professional development. She eventually applied to do her social work degree.

Claudia: Wow. I guess you might have inspired her. Let's talk about your lightbulb moment. What would you say was your greatest?

Sharda: Although I've a 30-year career in social work, that lightbulb moment didn't come until I was being coached in 2017. It was when I was exploring the subject of forgiveness.

I was saying, 'Yeah, yeah, I understand about forgiveness,' but my heart didn't. And although I said I'd forgiven the people I needed

---

11 Initial Response Teams deal with all telephone contacts and referrals for children and young people across a town/city who do not have an allocated social worker.

to forgive, the truth is that I hadn't. But the whole thing about forgiveness came as a lightbulb moment. And one day, I totally got it.

From that lightbulb moment, I learned how important it was to forgive people. Even if they didn't even know that I'd forgiven them, it is still part of my healing process. And once I'd consciously forgiven, I was able to then move on from the experience that was holding me back and avoid getting stuck in a difficult situation. I was able to deal with it and then say, 'I've encountered that, and I've grown and learned from it.' That forgiveness helped me form a career path that wasn't necessarily aspirational because I no longer wanted to be a director, something I'd previously aspired to do. Just because you're not seeking heights doesn't mean that you're any less or more valuable. The whole forgiveness thing helped me decide what I truly wanted. I couldn't have done that without forgiveness because it meant that I'm done with proving myself.

Claudia: That's great, Sharda, because having to continually prove yourself requires a lot of energy and often resources. What would you say was the most crucial resource on your journey?

Sharda: The most crucial resources were some insightful people who gave me the ability to reflect and understand what reflection really meant. One was Tony Morrison, a staff supervision guru. Interestingly, I received a text from him that said, 'Hi Sharda, I'm a bit busy at the moment. I'll call you in a couple of weeks.' He died in those two weeks, and I kept that text for over a year. He saw the spark in me. He asked me to join his team of trainers responsible for training managers of new Newly Qualified Social Workers.

Just being in the same room as Tony, you felt as though you were learning something. He was very warm, caring, and nurturing. He taught me the true meaning of empathic practice, emotional intelligence, self-awareness, and reflection on what you do. He was also the supervisor in my head. So if I asked myself, 'What would Tony say right now?' I would know the answers. What a loss!

I used to sit on the local safeguarding children board with the Director of Social Services. She also saw a spark in me and gave me opportunities that other senior managers in partnering agencies would question. But she didn't just throw me in the deep end; she gave me opportunities that really stretched me. For example, she asked me to chair a Serious Case Review for the first time, and nobody thought I was up to it. She just said, 'You'll be alright; you'll do it well.' And I learned and developed.

As a white woman, she'd chosen to work in this city because of her understanding of discrimination. This was a city that had more disabled children than its statistical neighbours. So she was a real advocate for equality. She ensured that disadvantaged children had equal access. She understood it and helped me to understand it, too. Despite her senior role, she always remembered the child at the centre of everything we did.

The third person was a Pakistani woman who qualified in social work after me and quickly rose into management. I think her brain was much more directed into management, so she didn't practice in frontline social work for long and became Head of Safeguarding. I saw a lot of myself in her passion and enthusiasm and her no-nonsense approach.

She was the first Asian person to attain a similar status as mine within the organisation. Somebody I could have a giggle with and share stories about Indian mothers, and we didn't have to finish the sentences because we both got it. Or the line of, 'I went to a wedding this weekend...' Every Indian or Pakistani person knows what Indian and Pakistani weddings are like. So we didn't have to finish those sentences. You can't have those cultural conversations with people you manage. And the only South Asian people I worked with on a day-to-day basis in this organisation were the ones that I managed.

She was somebody that was in my life for just a short while but helped me put things in perspective and make sense of it. It's interesting, isn't it? Because I'm sure you must have had white people say to you, 'Claudia, what's it like to be black?' I've certainly had lots of people say it to me. Certainly, when I was working in those social work cases with Asian families, colleagues would ask, 'What's it like to be an Indian woman in social work?' Well, I have nothing else to compare it with. This is who I am. And when I asked them, 'Tell me what it's like to be a white social worker and then we can perhaps have the conversation,' They would look shocked and horrified as if I should know. So, yeah, it's all of that. It's about being with somebody who you don't have to explain yourself to.

Throughout my career, I've had some great white managers; I've had some awful managers, too. But I've always had to explain a little bit to them about the nature and impact of prejudice. It became so exhausting.

Claudia: Let's move on to the subject of leadership. What do you understand by it?

Sharda: Good leadership is forming a relationship with the people you lead so that they trust you to do your job well. Good leaders make the most of the strengths of those they lead. They model good behaviour and are willing to work as hard as their followers.

Good leaders are aware that their staff might know more than they do because they are doing a different job from the leader. So, for example, I used to be responsible for a domestic abuse project for Pakistani women. Clearly, as a social worker, I understood the issues around domestic abuse and the impact on children, although I've never specifically worked in that area. Because my team had worked in the area of domestic abuse and knew a lot about it, their impact on the project was far greater. And that was okay because they were the practitioners. I was the manager and leader.

And whilst a leader should trust her staff to do the job, she should also ensure that they trust her to manage and lead them to do a good job. So, it's having really clear role boundaries and a relationship based on trust, honesty and integrity. Good leaders recognise all the contributors and understand their individual development needs. They help you stretch, grow and learn.

Good leaders also create space for those they lead to show their vulnerability, explore, and work it out. Leaders who make it comfortable and permissible to talk about worries and concerns are able to empower workers who become creative, tenacious, and hardworking. Good leaders cover the backs of people they lead, too. I would always say to those I managed, 'If you've done something wrong, I should be the first person that you tell because I'll be the one that helps you get out of it. So, as soon as you've done something, let's talk about it and be really open and positive about those conversations.' And, although I had to discipline or put action plans in place sometimes, it was always for the good of the service and the benefit of the children we were serving.

Good leaders also support people to stretch themselves; punch above their weight. And good leaders will stretch themselves, too, and model that behaviour.

Good leaders are authoritative. But they also care. And they pay attention and are responsive. They aren't neglectful, and they aren't authoritarian dictators. It's a bit like being a good parent, isn't it? They set the rules, clarify the boundaries, state what's expected of those they lead and of themselves. But with that comes warmth and caring and getting the balance right.

A good leader recognises, praises, and rewards good work and offers incentives. For example, when I was a middle manager, I had a team member who desperately wanted to do a particular course. It wasn't that expensive, but it was quite time-consuming for a short period. As she had done some excellent work, I negotiated with senior management for space and time to enable her to do the course.

Also, a good leader will hold her hand up when she's done something wrong and say she's sorry. Since being involved in some serious case reviews, I've moved away from blame. Even when staff have said, 'I've messed up; I've done something wrong.' It was never about blame. It was about, 'Okay, how do we undo it? How do we recover? And how do we make sure that you don't do it again?' These are lessons to be learned. Reprimanding isn't helpful to anybody.

The current director of my local authority operates very much in that style. She's the sort of woman who'll give you a hug even though you don't expect directors to hug. And she's the sort of person that tells you off, and you thank her for it at the end of the conversation because she's explained it really well to you. But she's also really clear where you're out of order, where it's unacceptable; this is what we're going to do about it. You end up thanking her.

I've been really inspired by Michelle Obama these days. I'm reading a lot about her humility. She's definitely a woman of influence. And, of course, Barack, I suppose, in terms of black men. This sounds really odd because, of course, he's always black in the way that I'm always black, but knowing when not to use my colour. Knowing when it's a black issue and when it isn't.

Claudia: So, as an Asian woman, what have you brought to your leadership roles?

Sharda: I've brought insight into what it's like to constantly struggle through institutionalised discrimination and not just institutionalised, sometimes outright, discrimination and work through it with some success.

One of my greatest achievements has been mentoring other black practitioners into management roles. I was never mentored into management, and it would have been really lovely, helpful, and supportive. I didn't have any positive black role models in my career. There was an academic programme that started in one of the London health trusts that tried to help black managers progress within the health service and break through that glass ceiling. You couldn't do this course without having a black mentor. I was a mentor on this programme of six up-and-coming managers within my organisation.

I helped them to understand that balance of knowing when to speak about their identity and when to be the social worker. We all have different identities, don't we? I'm a woman, a mum, a grandma, and I'm Indian. Some identities are more prominent in different situations. I'm always a woman, but, in some situations, you just need to be a person, a member of the human race and your gender is irrelevant. When I'm chairing my fostering panel, I'm the chair of the fostering panel. I occasionally work or listen to a case of a black child or black carers. So I become a woman of colour with that insight. So, you use it at different times. You have to get that balance right. I think women have to do it, but also women of colour or people of colour have to do it more in terms of their identity. Mentoring other black managers coming into the organisation, I've been able to have those conversations. Being able to have those conversations with someone who shares your experiences without having to explain everything is really helpful.

Claudia: And now the final question: our top three tips for women of colour who want to lead in their field. What are they?

Sharda: It's hard to be a woman and become successful. To be a woman of colour and strive for success is triple hard. So, my top tip would be to do what you enjoy and be clear on the underpinning purpose. Don't do it if you don't enjoy it or don't know the purpose of it. You'll be more successful if you enjoy it, and you'll work harder at it and put passion into it. Where passion, skills, and experience collide, you're going to get a much better outcome. My advice for any woman of colour, if you want to be successful, do what you enjoy and put the effort in. And when you no longer enjoy doing it, stop doing it.

It's about when passion and purpose and your value base intersect. Those are what motivate you. When I go for job interviews now, and they ask, 'What skills do you bring?' I say, 'Before I tell you about my skills and experience, let me tell you about my underlying values, why I do it, and what motivates me.' That's why I've stayed in social work for this length of time because I truly believe that people like me who can make a positive difference in children's lives should be making a difference.

And my second tip is to find a good coach or mentor. Somebody that will juggle your brain and really get you thinking; somebody whose shoulder you can lean on and who will support you and guide you if you get it wrong. Also, someone who will hold you to account and push you a bit further, and someone who will kick your butt when needed. They will help you stay true to your principles and your purpose because they'll make you reflect. The coach, the mentor, the person that helps you scratch your head doesn't have the answers; you have the answers. But somebody that stretches you and gets you thinking, I guess, will help you find your answers and make sure that you continue to do things that you want to do and enjoy doing and keep you purposeful.

My third tip is to punch above your weight. If you've somebody you can rely on, who's there for you, and supports you, you can stretch and punch above your weight. If you punch above your weight and you succeed, it will increase your confidence and help you do more challenging things and stretch yourself further. If you don't succeed, it's okay. Learn from it.

'It's hard to be a woman and become successful. To be a woman of colour and strive for success is triple hard. So, my top tip would be, to do what you enjoy and be clear on the underpinning purpose.'

— Sharda

CHAPTER 3

Mandu: The Political Party Leader

Here's the scenario: You're a child of rebels; rebels who got together when the apartheid world was screaming 'forbidden', and the anti-apartheid world was just as unwelcoming. You grow up with a burgeoning awareness of the power of injustice, the varied limits it heaps on black lives, and the multitude of privileges it affords white lives. And, from witnessing the individual and sharply contrasting experiences of your rebel parents, you begin to develop a well-honed antenna to inequality and the difference that racial identity makes. Inevitably, you identify with the struggle for racial justice. Considering all of that, what are the odds against you taking a leaf from your parents' playbook and becoming a rebel, too?

If you believe that your background shapes your life, you would also be given a tow to agree that powerful childhood experiences can influence your career trajectory. And so, it came to be for this Page 1 Woman, Mandu Reid: a smart, perceptive, enthusiastic, honest, and courageous rebel. An angry black woman who, like most black women, has much to be angry about this dominant stereotype.

Mandu didn't plan for a political career. Becoming a party leader wasn't even an afterthought—there were no blueprints for black British women in this role, after all. The degree she chose, together with her subsequent careers, brought her nearer to the seats of power. Perhaps, unconsciously at least, she was developing her skills and knowledge and possibly mapping out the territory on her journey towards political leadership.

Mandu was named by Apolitical as a member of the global Gender Equality Top 100 (2019) (alongside the likes of Christine Lagarde, Ruth Bader Ginsburg, Michelle Obama, and Nancy Pelosi), which, you have to agree, is a long unthinkable shot, particularly when you have just been a party leader for less than a year. When a black woman pioneer comes along and makes such an outstanding mark at supersonic speed, one cannot help but wonder what other surprises await us. Let's find out.

THE INTERVIEW

Claudia: Mandu, tell us what you do.

Mandu: I'm the leader of the UK Women's Equality Party. We are the first and only UK feminist political party, and we are merely five years old. In some way, we're the new kid on the block when it comes to UK politics. Our purpose is to make sure that equality between men and women is prioritised—front and centre. No other political party in the history of British politics has ever succeeded in doing that. None of the other parties, despite what they say, are anywhere near ambitious enough about this form of equality. They may talk about it, but examine what they actually do, how they do it, and, crucially, what they don't do. You'll have the evidence you need to ascertain that equality often gets relegated to a footnote in their manifestos or their priorities.

I used to be a member of the Labour Party. Although my experience was not altogether negative, I eventually felt disappointment and deep resentment that the party of equality couldn't bring itself to truly prioritise one of the most enduring forms of inequalities that's prevalent in this country and worldwide. I wanted to put my energy and my passion into something that recognised the front-and-centre importance of this issue. That's how I initially got interested in the Women's Equality Party.

And here's a bit of trivia for you: I'm the first person of colour ever to lead a national political party in the UK. That's pretty shocking when you think about it. We're not Denmark, where there are hardly any black people. We are the UK. We have a colonial history. A history of immigration. A history of relationships with countries worldwide, countries we once dominated. We're a place steeped in diversity. Yet, in the history of politics, in the major political parties, the Tory party, which is nearly 200 years old, and the Labour party, about 120 years old, not a single woman or man of colour has ever occupied the position of party leader. Why hasn't the Labour Party, the exalted party of equality, managed it? Its last leadership contest had four women and one man in the race. They chose, in their wisdom, to elect (just for a change!) another white, middle-aged, Oxbridge-educated, male lawyer to be their party leader. Another one! I'm not saying there's anything intrinsically wrong with him—that's not the point. The point is that there are huge barriers to women and black people in political leadership. For black women, it's a double whammy.

On some levels, my work is about demonstrating that it is possible and, consequently, signalling to other black women that they don't have to accept the role of 'bridesmaid' or second fiddle, and indefinitely being in a position of having to wait for their turn. We can take our power. We can use our voice. That's a big part of my job. It's about demonstrating all of that and trying to set an example.

I also ran for the Mayor of London in 2021. The hustings on International Women's Day 2020, the first major hustings of the campaign, was a huge moment for me. To be honest, on that day, I felt a lot of pressure, felt intimidated on a large scale, felt what I think a lot of black women feel when they're trying to take up space in environments where nobody expects them to be. And those all-too-familiar comments along the lines of 'How wonderful that you made it this far' are, in my view, backhanded compliments.

I worked hard for it. I really did. I often say this about women and about black women in leadership or any part of life: that in our patriarchal environment, the culture, the systems, we often have to work twice as hard to get half as far. I could possibly say that my knowledge of the subject relevant to that debate was sharper and super-intelligent than most of the other candidates. They were much more seasoned politicians earning much more than I do. They have been in this game for decades and amassed enormous teams. I could tell by their introductory speeches, most of which were obviously generic, that equality between men and women was not a prioritised endeavour for them. For example, Rory Stewart, the most high-profile candidate (apart from the mayor candidate). He went to Eton and was a cabinet minister in Theresa May's government. He eventually stood down from the race, but his speech was very generic, very off-the-shelf—although it wasn't bad. He talked about London as a miracle. I had heard him do that speech everywhere he went on the campaign trail. And I thought, 'No, this is the International Women's Day hustings. Use your brain-power to make what you have to say relevant to this audience.'

Claudia: It's interesting that in the equality field, the initiative for a women's equality party came before a disabled equality party, or a people of colour equality party, or an LGBTQ+ equality party. Why do you think that is?

Mandu: In some respects, the Women's Equality Party is the party of those other intersections as well. It's in our DNA, it's in our founding documents, it's in the principles that we adhere to by recognising the intersections of people's identities. We acknowledge that these things matter and need to be highlighted and that policy is needed to address them. So, for example, if you are a black woman with a disability, you've got three layers of oppression to navigate.

Why are we the Women's Equality Party? Because its founders were reacting to sexism, to the multiple ways in which men and women have for millennia operated under the hierarchy where women are at the nadir and oftentimes tagged a worthy subordinate to men in terms of status, quality of life, and ability to live freely and achieve their potential to the fullest. That was their starting point. It could easily have been a People of Colour Equality Party if racism was the starting point. But no, it began because people contemplated the injustice that was initiated by male supremacy. That's the crux of our genesis: people with a shared experience of the challenges of being a woman came together and built a movement with that as its starting point.

Claudia: Did you ever have a personal vision or a plan of leading a political party, or did you reach here by accident, as it were?

Mandu: I'm going to be honest. I could never have predicted that this would be what I would be doing. I'm not one of those people who had a plan to be a political leader by any stretch of imagination. But I've been reflecting on this, and I guess you could argue that on my journey through life I've had experiences that have conspired to prepare me for this position.

Let's go way back to the very beginning. I was born in 1981 in Malawi. My mother is a black Malawian woman. My father is a white British man. And they met in the 1970s. At that time, there was a bulk of controversy about them being a mixed-race couple. It was a huge disappointment to my father's family. His father and mother effectively threatened to disown him. My parents got married in Malawi, and his father boycotted the wedding. My father's mother came in the end, but not after she'd written my father many, many letters using the analogy of swans and blackbirds and how swans and blackbirds don't mate, and how it doesn't work even if they eventually do. If you're a swan, you need to find another swan. That was her narrative.

People in my mother's community were much more laid back and certainly not as hostile, but they weren't exactly delighted either. When you think about it, the genesis of my life was this union between my mother and father that resulted in most people being disappointed by it to some degree. In effect, becoming a married couple, in that context, was a rebellious act. In a way, that's the origin story, right? I exist because, in some respect, there was a rebellion against the status quo. And my mother and father embodied that rebellion.

My father was not a diplomatic grandstanding type of guy (like many British 'expatriates' of his generation). He was an English teacher who worked in various countries. I spent most of my childhood from age five in what was then known as Swaziland, now called Eswatini. It's a little landlocked country that shares most of its borders with South Africa. Those were the twilight years of apartheid South Africa. So, even though my family wasn't active politically, our very existence was politically significant.

I remember one trip from Swaziland by car to Durban on the South African coast. It was a ten-hour drive, and we had to stop over at a petrol station somewhere to put gas in the car, wash the windscreen, and use the loo. We had to go into three different toilets. The toilet that my mother was allowed to use was the most shabby and nasty. The one that me and my sister, as mixed-race children, were allowed to use, was a bit better. The one that my father used was clean and well-tended. As a young child at the time, I was baffled by that. I didn't know exactly the ins and outs of structural oppression. But this is one of my sharpest memories from my childhood. I was a young child, but I could perceive the stink of injustice. And because South Africa was the backdrop, although we were in Swaziland, which was like a little island of resistance to South Africa, apartheid permeated everything.

Racial inequality was the struggle that I identified with most profoundly when I was very young. So, again, the seeds were being sown for me to be alert to inequality. This was particularly significant for me because I'm a mixture of two people who, as a result of the inequality, should be on opposing sides of the racial divide, at least on paper.

By the way, going back to my grandparents, my grandfather died when I was two, so I didn't get a chance to build a relationship with him. But over the years, I formed an incredible bond with my grandmother. My politics were informed by her change of heart and her acceptance of us because I believe that most people can change their views. The kind of politics I reject is the kind that is characterised by people digging trenches and planting themselves there, throwing grenades and crap at each other, and no progress happens. So, my politics is definitely underpinned by the belief that I can learn something from people that I disagree with, and they can learn something from me, and that it's essential to create spaces and opportunities that enable such mutual learning.

To me, truth and reconciliation are very important; people acknowledging trauma and trying to heal from it and people who have caused other people pain, accepting what they've done. This is incredibly healing. But we don't see enough of that in today's politics. It's very adversarial, tribal, and polarised. It's one of the questions I constantly wrestle with: how do I bring these values into what we do while staying relevant? Even though I haven't gotten the answer yet, I'm always working on it.

An interesting fact about me is that I definitely consider myself a latecomer to feminism. I only identified as a feminist from when I was about 26. And that was because I thought feminism was unnecessary until that point. I was one of those people that saw feminism as the dirty F word. I was uncomfortable with it and kind of hostile to it. That may be because of my background, where the focus was much more on racial injustice. I'm also of a generation where a lot of women my age reached young adulthood and were fed the lie that 'the work has been done... we can be educated now—all the way up to university level—we've got the vote, etc., 'Mission Equality' has been accomplished.'

Lad culture prevailed through my adolescence and young adulthood. It was one of the smoke screens that led me to believe that injustice and inequality between men and women, and male supremacy, were things of the past. So, until my mid-20s, I thought that feminism wasn't for me, and it wasn't necessary—that it was potentially nonsense. Anyway, I changed my mind, as I'm sure you can see. I look at young women now, and they have a much higher consciousness around feminism than I did when I was in my late teens or early 20s, which can only be a good thing! Essentially, I went through my 20s and 30s, working primarily in government environments as a civil servant. I worked for the treasury and the Department for Culture, Media, and Sports, and for all three mayors of London—Ken Livingstone, Boris Johnson, and Sadiq Khan. I've always been very politically aware, but I wasn't particularly active until the 2010 election when the Tory party was elected and formed the coalition government with the Lib Dems. That was on the back of the 2008 financial crisis, and I knew they would slash and burn public services.

I studied Social Policy and Government at the London School of Economics. So, I'm kind of versed in what the government's job is in terms of looking after its people and all of that stuff. I knew that there was a massive risk of public services being burnt to the ground, and this government wouldn't be at all shy about doing that. Conventional approaches to managing the economy give two alternatives when there's an economic crisis like that: you can pursue a strategy to grow the economy to get out of the crisis or cut public funding to essential services. The latter is what the Conservative / Lib Dem coalition did. If you think cutting public services is a good idea, you'd have been incredibly proud of that government. I was terrified about what they were going to do, and I joined the Labour party.

I live in a part of Southeast London, one of the capital's most diverse areas. There's a really high concentration of black people from African and Caribbean origin and other migrant populations. I was so excited to join the local Labour party and play my part in resisting the Tory coalition. But I remember being disappointed and surprised because, at that time, my local Labour party seemed to be dominated by white middle-class people who appeared to be several steps removed from the people who most needed the party to fight on their behalf. My area is a bright-red guaranteed Labour strong-hold, with all three MPs: Labour, Labour, Labour—big majorities: the local council, Labour, Labour, Labour. So there wasn't a sense of them being very responsive to local people because, actually, they didn't need to be. They were going to win every election whether they did a good job or not. It just put me off. Complacent politics wasn't the politics I wanted to be part of. So I left, and I thought, 'I'll never join another political party.'

Then, in 2015, the Women's Equality Party came along, and it sounded interesting. By then, I did consider myself a feminist. But I didn't want to join the cause. I thought it was a great idea, and I wanted to support what they did from the sidelines and help spread the word. But I didn't want to be a member because I was done with political party membership. That started to change when I learned more about our policies, in particular our Equal Parenting and Caregiving policies, which resonated with me in a very personal way.

When I was 33, I accidentally got pregnant. I wasn't in a proper relationship with the guy who was quite a bit younger than me. We looked at what we were going to do about it, and neither of us could imagine a situation where I wasn't going to be the sole or main caregiver of the child. I had a better job and earned more than he did. That's contrary to one of the explanations that are most com-monly given by heterosexual couples to explain why men don't carry out the main caregiver role. But it was the reverse in my case—and the presumption was that the caregiving role would fall to me, by default. In the end, I had to make a choice. I considered all the plans and ambitions I had for my life, and when it came down to it, I just didn't believe that I would have the mental resilience, the strength, the financial capability to be a single mother at that time. So I had an abortion.

That's why, a couple of years later, when I learned about the Woman's Equality Party's policies for Equal Parenting and Caregiving, I instantly understood how important they were. If properly shared parental leave and universal free childcare up to age five were national policies, I would have been able to make a different choice. So I wouldn't have had to sacrifice my career and the contribution I wanted to make to my community in order to become a mother. Even though we weren't together, with our shared parental leave policy, the father and I could have made a deal where he does half the childcare while the baby was small to make it fairer and more balanced. And my career wouldn't have to be totally derailed. In that moment, I realised the true importance of what the Women's Equality Party was fighting for, and I wanted to be part of it— integrally part of it.

I joined the party, and then I had this crazy experience of standing for election twice in close succession and then being elected spokesperson for Equal Parenting and Caregiving. Then our party leader stood down by surprise. I definitely didn't have a plan to become a party leader. But following my instincts and convictions, as well as having a background that had radicalised me and made me furious about inequality led me to where I was and to where I am now.

Claudia: So you followed your instincts and was led to where you are now. Would you say that you took some crucial steps, too?

Mandu: I've already talked about rebellion, haven't I? Despite what people often presume about me, possibly due to how I come across, like many of my sisters around the world, self-doubt is a strong feature of how I see myself and my potential. So one of the really important steps I took that changed my trajectory was closing my eyes, taking a deep breath, and rejecting self-doubt.

The first time I stood for a parliamentary election, the Lewisham East by-election was in 2018. By then, I was a member of the Party, and I was enjoying it. It felt good to cheerlead on the sidelines, to show my support, and wave a placard every now and then. But when the prospect came of actually being the figurehead of a local campaign and putting myself forward for election, I felt intimidated by it. I didn't believe that I could do justice to my party, to women, or black women. I remember feeling a crippling avalanche of self-doubt. I had to sit myself down and advise myself that if I pander to that self-doubt, I'd never know whether or not I'm any good at this. I didn't want to look back when I'm 90-years-old and regret never finding out or taking the opportunity to make a difference. When my mindset shifted from allowing self-doubt to influence my thinking, all sorts of doors opened for me. I was scared, I really was. Before that, whenever I had to do public speaking, I'd feel my heart beating fast inside my chest, threatening to pop out. But, somehow, serious preparation and actively saying to myself that self-doubt wouldn't help me or anyone else transformed my mindset. I still wrestle with it, but if I hadn't stood in that election, my trajectory would have been very different. I certainly wouldn't be the party leader. I wouldn't have had such rapid personal growth. I wouldn't have learned what my political and professional instincts are, and I wouldn't set an example for others who need to see people who resemble them at that level.

A really important part of that whole experience was that some-body asked me to stand. And, at that point, this long experience of wrestling with self-doubt kicked in. But this is a key thing because one of the things I've learned is that a way to uplift other women is to offer opportunities and show that you believe in them. If nobody had done that with me, I wouldn't have taken the next step, which was to deal with my personal battle with self-doubt.

So my learning is that self-doubt exists, so I had to wrestle it to the ground and rebel against it. It's due to what I've been taught. As women, we have been brainwashed since we were babies that we're of a lower status and social standing than our male counterparts— double whammy if you're a black woman. But it's not real, although it feels real. We must recognise it as fiction, something inexistent yet existing, and overcome it. We must find other people that we can each encourage and believe in and give them a chance. And we must support and not be hard on them if they're slow to take up our offer because it may take a while for their confidence to build.

I overcame self-doubt by examining what I stood to gain by becoming a party leader. I'm a curious person who craves new experiences. I have a strong sense of adventure. So, I framed the experience that I was likely to have in those terms. I also did my best to prepare and absorb as much learning as I could. I know none of these things are particularly ground-breaking, but it's what I did. I didn't have a five-step plan, but I took a risk. And I realised that the worst thing that could happen was nowhere near as important as the best thing that could happen as a result of it.

When I distilled it down, the worst thing that could have happened was a bit of embarrassment. And the best thing that could have happened was a sense of adventure, opportunities, personal growth, learning a whole lot of new things, and becoming a visible black woman in politics where black women were utterly absent. All of that stuff. I realised that I could fill a room with the things I could gain and maybe a matchbox with the stuff I was afraid of. It taught me a big lesson—that we are somehow preconditioned to give undue emphasis on things that scare us. It took me until my 30s to realise that truth.

Claudia: You won't have got to party leadership without facing challenges along the way. What was your greatest challenge, and how did you overcome it?

Mandu: I've had quite a few challenges. At first, people had low expectations of me. I learned to turn that to my advantage in politics. It can be really helpful if people underestimate you because it means that they don't see you as a threat. Before they realise you're potentially a threat, you've made some headway. As a younger woman, I found it very demoralising when people said things like, 'Gosh, you're so well-spoken.'

My mother is a PA for executives in big investment banks. I remember when I was a student at the LSE, she told me people were absolutely astonished that she had a daughter at one of the better universities in the country. She would tell me with a combination of frustration and pride. Maybe this contributed to my self-doubt because I couldn't work out why people thought it strange that I was studying at the London School of Economics. 'Is it a fluke?' I had asked myself. Now I see things differently. I've learned as well that there are many people who have done well in politics that are not that impressive. They really aren't.

Another challenge is being in a situation where I've sometimes felt like I'm representing all the black women that ever existed.

What's challenging here is the assumption that all black women are the same. It's like we're not real human beings with different views or preferences, different desires, hopes, dreams, whatever. Because I'm a black woman, I'm supposed to be the spokesperson or representative of all black women. I don't enjoy that.

I've struggled with that framing of black women because it reduces our humanity. I find myself second-guessing myself in unhelpful ways when I get frustrated and lose my temper. I've worried that I'll become the stereotype of the angry black woman rather than a person who is frustrated and has lost their temper for good reason. Because there are few black women in politics and even less in political leadership, the stakes are high, but the margin for error feels very small. If you are a public school-educated white guy who studied law at Oxford and then went on to become a lawyer, the stakes are much lower because there are many people like you who have already proven themselves, so you have automatic credentials. And the margin for error is much bigger. Look at what our prime minister is doing; he can fool around, not take things seriously, make fatal errors and get away with it. Imagine if it was a black woman who had stood up during a press conference in the middle of a pandemic and boasted about going into a hospital and shaking everybody's hand, including COVID-19 patients. She wouldn't be given a chance to say, 'Oops, that was careless.' He doesn't even have to say, 'Oops, that's careless' because, if you are in that dominant category, you don't have to apologise or explain yourself. You don't have to watch your back or your step. If you're a black woman, you have to do all of that stuff constantly, and it's draining. It drains mental and emotional energy. If I'm going to do this work, I must accept that these challenges are priced in. But I also want people to understand that it's not right that they are priced in.

Overcoming these challenges is a work in progress. I take lots of deep breaths. There's a tip I borrowed from Julia Gillard, ex-prime minister of Australia. At the very start of her term as prime minister, she wrote on a piece of paper the reasons why she was doing the job and what she wanted to achieve. She folded the paper, put it in her handbag, and moved it every time she changed handbags. By the end of her time as prime minister, it was a ragged, sweaty, grubby scrap of paper. She said it helped her remember what she was there to achieve and do when the going got tough. It helped her stay true to herself.

I have a similar practice. When I'm doubting myself, when I'm fearful of making a misstep, or facing a dilemma, for example—should we push for a policy to nationalise childcare, or should we worry that it will upset small business owners? I go back to my purpose, what I'm there to achieve. I've not written it on a piece of paper, but I usually take myself away quietly, and I'll ask myself, 'Why am I doing this?' And this reflection and self-questioning re-centres me. It increases my fortitude to face people's criticisms and suspicions, my own suspicions of myself and of feeling unworthy. It's a small thing inspired by Julia Gillard. More women should do the same thing because it's easy to get caught up in criticism, the risk you feel you're taking, and the fear of getting something wrong.

To convince myself to stand for the election that first time, I had to remind myself of the benefits, which far outweighed the negatives. There are times when it's stressful and intense, like an election campaign, and I have to remind myself more. Or maybe if I was going to be on 'Question Time'. If you ever see me on 'Question Time', I would be so full of adrenaline and fretful anticipation in the run-up because of my fear of making a mistake, or the margin for error is so small and the stakes being so high. But I will use that technique of, 'Why does it matter? Why am I doing this job? What am I hoping for in the long run?' Even if I make a misstep now, it doesn't mean that I can't steer back on course.

Claudia: I'm assuming that a journey like yours would have been full of lightbulb moments, right? What was your particular lightbulb moment?

Mandu: If we're talking about my lightbulb moment in relation to where I am now as leader of the Women's Equality Party, it was more of 'a stitch-up moment' than a lightbulb moment. When I realised there was a stitch-up against women, it was me accidentally getting pregnant and realising that, even if this man and I played an equal part in creating this baby, the responsibility for caring for it would disproportionately be mine. It doesn't matter that I'm a well-educated woman living a relatively privileged life in London; his life wasn't going to be diverted off course by becoming a parent in the same way that mine would've been. But it doesn't have to be that way.

I struggle to separate being a woman from being a black woman and what part the latter played in shaping my journey because the two are intertwined.

I think it's doubly important for black women to be seen achieving and living fulfilling lives. So being a black woman did play an indirect part in the lightbulb or stitch-up moment related to my decision in the face of an unplanned pregnancy in my 30s. I felt that if I sacrificed my dreams and ambitions, I would be playing into the narrative that women have all been socialised to believe that they are ultimately inferior. But here's the caveat: I am in awe of the thousands of black women, white women, whatever race, who have succeeded as single mothers, brought up a family by themselves, and who have managed to keep their careers on track, even started businesses or whatever it might be. I just didn't feel that I had the strength to do it.

Claudia: Let's talk about resources now. What resources have been crucial to your success?

Mandu: I think about resources in terms of hardware (i.e. technical and infrastructure-based stuff) and software (for example, my relationships and people that have advised or listened to me or opened doors for me). I've not had doors opened for me by powerful people, but I have had people introduce me to others who have been undeniably helpful. So the resources that have made the biggest difference have been more on the software side, where I've had people in my corner who have encouraged me helped me build my confidence and my voice, who have given me the benefit of their experience and wisdom. The most significant people have been women I didn't actively seek out. I've never had a formal mentor, but I've had encouragement and support from women in lots of different ways. This has made all of the difference to me.

We often underestimate the value of connectors. You can make a transformative difference to somebody's career success, to somebody's confidence, and trajectory in life by being a connector and being prepared to take a risk on someone. I always try to connect people to other people I know rather than letting 'jealousy' guard my connections. When you're starting out and you didn't go to Eton or take any of those prestigious elite pathways to success where they teach you how to network, it can be tough. That's why they have things like the Burlington Club or sororities and fraternities in the States because they enable good networking.

I believe you have a duty if you are successful to help connect other people and take the reputational risk of doing so because not being as well-connected (on average) is one of the things that we as black women have stacked against us. Most of us are not from environments where our networks gave us an easy pathway to the places we're trying to get into throughout our childhood, school years, and adulthood. Even when we're in certain environments where networking happens, we're not always welcome. We're sometimes frozen out because our face doesn't fit the mainstream. So I'm quite deliberate about taking a risk on people, even if there's a chance of it potentially reflecting a little bit badly on me if they turn out to be problematic or a bit of a disappointment.

Claudia: I'd like to ask you about your charity that you've not mentioned, but which I've heard about, The Cup Effect. Tell us about it.

Mandu: Well, I discovered a particular solution to menstruation, the menstrual cup. They've been around since the 1930s but are not a high-profile mainstream product. They're more comfortable, more reliable, more convenient, and they save you money. They're better for the planet because you only need one, and you literally reuse the same one for 10 years. Now, I thought that sounded like an awful idea when I first encountered it. But when I tried it, it improved my quality of life.

My mother grew up in a rural part of Malawi and spent much of her childhood living in poverty-stricken conditions. Her family has a very different status in Malawi now, but when she was a child, there was no way she would have been considered middle class.

When my mother started her period, she had an awful time because nobody there could afford tampons or pads. They had to use pieces of cloth that were uncomfortable and unhygienic. If she had had access to menstrual cups, it would have transformed her experience. She would have been able to participate in everyday life, go to school confidently, and be herself.

I was wondering why I, a well-educated woman, brought up in Southern Africa and the UK hadn't learned about the menstrual cup until I was 26. And here's the reason: pads and tampons are incredibly lucrative, and big corporations make a killing out of them. It doesn't matter to them what might be more comfortable or convenient for women and girls or what's better for the planet. What matters to them is their profit margin.

I founded the charity 'The Cup Effect', on the premise that the menstrual cup could be a gamechanger for millions of women and girls in parts of the world where poverty prevails. My charity has raised awareness about menstrual cups, run training courses, and made them available to women and girls in communities where they wouldn't have otherwise been accessible. And you can take a girl throughout an entire educational career with one menstrual cup. It's about informed choice. We have never imposed anything on anyone; our mission is to give women and girls more options.

Claudia: As a party leader and as the founder of a charity, you'll definitely have a view on leadership. What do you understand by it?

Mandu: Leadership has key ingredients: setting an example; taking responsibility; setting direction; mobilising, enabling, empowering, inspiring and motivating others; and taking risks. I've worked in environments throughout my career where I've either been working directly for or had proximity to a powerful leader. I worked for Ken Livingstone, Boris Johnson, and Sadiq Khan, for example. I worked directly for the permanent secretary of the Department of Culture, Media and Sport before I worked in City Hall. So I've seen different types of leaders in action.

Most days, I ask myself, 'Am I doing enough to set a positive example?' Sometimes I feel like I'm not, partly because of the nonsensical expectation of some people that I am supposed to represent all black women.

Setting direction is really important because you've got to take responsibility and give clarity to those you're leading about where they're going and how they'll get there. I enjoy that part of leadership, maybe because I'm the oldest child, and I've often felt responsible for problem-solving. So I'm someone who tries to take responsibility, sometimes a little bit too much. Setting direction in this job can be challenging because the Women's Equality Party has more than 30,000 members and supporters and 70 branches up and down the country. That's not a group of women who always agree or who have exactly the same priorities. Yet, I'm supposed to set direction in a way that does justice to enough people in the movement, so they know where we're going and if they want to come along.

The parts of leadership I feel most confident about are motivating, enabling, and empowering people. It's something I'm really passionate about. I love to see women finding their voices, their power, and their confidence. That's why I love our party conferences because they provide space for women to stand up and argue for what they believe in, something they've oftentimes never done before. One of my goals for the next five years is to enable thousands of women to find their voices and their power through what we're doing—black women in particular because we are often unwelcome in environments where that is happening.

And then you must be willing to take risks once you're leading change. You have to be prepared with enough thick skin—but not too thick or you might lose touch with people. It's important that you stay connected to what matters and doesn't matter to people, what upsets and motivates them. If your skin is too thick, likely, you won't retain that connectivity. On the contrary, if your skin is too thin, you won't have the audacity to take risks as you'll be terrified of criticism. Although criticism can be daunting, I like to be challenged. I hope I can create an environment where people are prepared to challenge me when necessary.

I'm constantly trying to find the right balance between those ingredients of leadership. I'm still on the learning curve with my own leadership journey. I hope that over the next few years, I become wiser and learn from my mistakes. Being self-aware and learning from mistakes are other important aspects of leadership.

Claudia: How are these leadership qualities relevant to you as a black woman, Mandu?

Mandu: They're relevant because I consciously measure myself against them. It's a framework I've been using privately that helps me establish where I've got things to work on and what I do quite well. Anyone can use it. In relation to black women, at the moment, it's very difficult being in a position of leadership because everything is moving so rapidly. COVID-19 came along and blew the whole world to pieces. It's creating specific challenges for black communities and black women in particular. And then we have the aftermath of the George Floyd protests. And what makes me uncomfortable as a leader right now is feeling behind the curve in terms of setting direction about our response to those grand issues.

I wake up, and it's the first thing I think about each morning. I go to sleep at night, and it's the last thing I think about. I'm a thoughtful person. But it's tough when everything is moving so fast to remain thoughtful and deliberate about what I'm doing rather than run to where the action is. If you were to ask which of those things I'm most insecure about right now, setting direction is what I want to sort out because of the urgency of what's going on and the catastrophic impact of COVID-19, particularly for black women and other marginalised groups, when the economic crisis bites. Even though there is pressure to run quickly out of the starting block, you don't always get the right answer if you are too knee-jerk in your response. I also look at other leaders like Jacinda Ardern, who's led New Zealand well throughout the pandemic. She knows how to set direction, and everyone can learn from her.

Claudia: You made mention of Jacinda Ardern, who has a great reputation as a leader and is a brilliant role model. Which black women leaders are your role models?

Mandu: There's Graca Machel, who's politically active, but she's not leading a country. I've met her, and I admire a lot of what she has done.

Stacy Abrams is her own woman. She was unashamed of putting forward an uber progressive agenda that centred on the experiences of black people in the state of Georgia. She's a really good communicator and open-minded about her background. She doesn't pretend that she's had a smooth life, and she's spoken openly about her debts.

There's always pressure on women to conform to certain templates, and even more so for black women. The conventional wisdom, especially for black women who face double standards, is to keep stuff like her personal debt under wraps. But she doesn't do that; she chooses to be real. Jacinda Arden is similar in as much as there was pressure on her to take a macho approach after the fatal attack on the Mosque. She didn't do that. She used her emotional intelligence to handle it. We'd get so much more out of women leaders, black or white, if they had permission to be themselves. Being unable to be ourselves is a real obstacle that holds us back. I don't want to set an example of trying to fit in because women who don't fit in need to be encouraged to come forward and take their chances as their authentic selves.

Claudia: I believe that you are increasingly being seen as a role model, and an ambitious black and Asian woman might value your advice. What three top tips would you give such women who want to be leaders in their field?

Mandu: I've been reading this book called *Radical Compassion*. The first tip is to extend radical compassion to yourself. Black girls have been socialised from the day we were born to zoom in on our flaws. That's not being compassionate to ourselves. Nobody is perfect, right? How many mediocre white men have made it to top positions? And so we don't have to be perfect at everything. Being compassionate to yourself is allowing yourself space to learn and grow and not chastising and demeaning yourself or wishing you were different. So extend radical compassion to yourself.

Number two, it's really important to have an open mind. Avoid making assumptions about people. Unlearn that because you never know who is going to be helpful or supportive of you. Sometimes a lifeline gets thrown from the place that you least expect it. So be open-minded.

And the third tip: deliberately and purposefully cultivate a mutually supportive community around you. And that doesn't have to be only with women of colour. It could be women from other backgrounds. You support them, they support you. You'll learn and grow that way. Investigate and find the ones that work for you or create your own. Remember that when you support other people, you'll get it back ten-fold, especially if you are part of a group. Imagine you spend a couple of hours helping one of your sisters in the group. Next time you need something, all ten women in your group would put two hours in, getting you back 20 hours of support and backup. That's one of the strongest antidotes to women's self-doubt, which, unless the world changes radically, women will absorb throughout their childhood, teenage years, and adulthood.

Black women are dealing with sexism, misogyny, male supremacy, white supremacy, racism, and colourism or issues around heritage. Overlay the two headlines, sexism and racism, and you get double jeopardy. So the sisterhood is doubly important because you'll always struggle to fulfil your potential if you're only ever in environments where you have to explain yourself. It's draining. We should be putting our energy into creativity, problem-solving, developing ourselves, and personal growth. But if I have to put half my energy into explaining why you shouldn't touch my hair or why 'all lives matter' is a problematic thing to say, that's not a good way of making the most of my time or of what I have to offer the world. So, yes, sisterhood applies to all women, but it applies double to black women because we're trying to navigate multiple oppressions.

'On some levels, my work is about demonstrating that it is possible and, consequently, signalling to other black women that they don't have to accept the role of 'bridesmaid' or second fiddle, and indefinitely being in a position of having to wait for their turn. We can take our power. We can use our voice.'

— Mandu

Su: Coach and Mentor for Human Resources

When you think of Human Resources (HR) professionals, what images spring to mind? HR is expected to be the 'people' people of an organisation, so I certainly would presume that they would be blessed with a high approval rating from staff and more widely. On the contrary, HR professionals are traditionally seen as the organisation's scary police or its pink and fluffy agony aunt—polar opposites. You have to wonder what they've done to deserve it. So I reckon that HR often gets bad press, right? But is this fair?

That's why my Page 1 Woman, Su Patel, an HR coach and mentor, is on a mission to transform the face of HR. 'I want to help HR professionals understand that we need to be a brand that enables businesses and their people to grow, rather than a brand that's restrictive and unclear about its role.' Designing her 'HR Brand Blueprint' was her first step towards achieving her mission. Not bad for the former Tesco checkout girl who became a manager at the age of 18.

So, who is Su Patel? She's smart, capable, with a clear vision and a clear head; a risk-taker who leads by building leaders. Given her deprived background, a childhood characterised by bullying, isolation, poor self-esteem, and divorced parents at a time when divorce was taboo in the Indian community, how did she transition from the check-out tills to creating an HR department? She may have had no HR training, but she had a commendable load of wisdom, determination, and ambition that enabled that well-known supermarket chain to develop engaged staff and a thriving business. And all this came to exist despite the cultural obstacles that continue to dog her from time to time. Financing herself through her HR courses and acquiring three properties before the age of 30 suggests a woman hell-bent on becoming something more.

Let's meet Su Patel.

THE INTERVIEW

Claudia: So, Su, describe what you do.

Su: HR isn't liked or respected by many people. I want to change its direction so that it is more credible, more respected and valued in organisations. So I am sharing my message about being more human, more inclusive, more understanding and compassionate in the workplace, but at the same time is balanced. There are many HR professionals who are either so people-focused that they forget about the business growth and policies. Or they are really great at all the policies, processes, and strategies but aren't great at looking after the people. HR is paid by the company to support the business. But, at the end of the day, supporting a business has to be done through engaging and recognising the people, which is necessary for them to perform well for the business.

I created my 'HR Brand Blueprint' programme to help HR professionals create more balance between the people and the business, providing a service to the business and being clear about why they are there. I focused on five areas: partnership, process, performance, productivity, and progress. It's really about getting that message out to HR professionals about how to be more balanced in their role and using the role to make a difference to people rather than because it ticks a box for their CV.

I coach, mentor, and train ambitious HR professionals who may be struggling in their roles or want to move up the career ladder. Often, HR professionals find it hard to be respected and valued in a business. So I run a training programme that gives them the confidence they need to have an impact on the business.

Clients come mainly through referrals. But I also use social media, videos, articles and interviews, and networking events to build relationships with people and share what I do. Through these videos and articles on social media, I've positioned myself as an authority in that field. Then there is my award-winning book, *Putting the Human Back into HR,* which is a great resource for that purpose. It has sold so well that I was invited to the HR convention by the Maldives Association for HR Professionals in 2019, where I gave a keynote on my book to an audience of 400 people.

I'm also one of the founders of The World Transformation Organisation, which was set up in 2018. My co-founders are Kalpesh Patel and Harinder Pau. Its purpose is to make personal development accessible to everybody worldwide. We started by opening up a personal development academy in a slum in India in 2018. Once a month, we have motivational speakers, yoga teachers, and trainers going in and providing the children and families with a bit of inspiration and motivation to help them realise that life doesn't have to be about poverty and desperation. They, too, can have dreams, and they, too, can realise them.

As well as that, we have World Transformation Day, which we started when we launched this academy. World Transformation Day happens every year on the first Sunday in April. It's like Valentine's Day, Father's Day, or Mother's Day when we have leaders from all over the world share their message with the world. They create videos and events to transform themselves or others in their communities. In the first year, we had about 45 leaders take part. They impacted nearly 12,000 people. In 2019, 123 leaders shared their message and impacted nearly 45,000 people. So, in 2020, our aim was to reach a million people.

I guess that becoming an entrepreneur after being an employee of 30 years at Tesco, I really get that the entrepreneurial life is all about making a difference and living a life that's about getting up to stuff that's bigger than you. We're really out for making a huge impact in the world to as many people as we can. They say that 'you rise by lifting others,' and that's what we're doing.

Claudia: So, how did you get into HR?

Su: I started my working life at the age of 16 as an enthusiastic checkout chick at Tesco. For the first time in my life, I felt a sense of belonging and got praised, encouraged, and recognised. So I really loved being at work. It was a great place for me to learn new skills and get acknowledged. So I developed and worked on my weaknesses and gradually set and improved my own work standards. I took on more responsibilities and tried things out.

I knew I could get promoted like the guys. My bosses saw me using my initiative, taking risks, and helping the business. So they supported me, and I developed my leadership skills. When I was 18, I was promoted and began managing older and more experienced colleagues. I also read my first leadership book, *How to Win Friends and Influence People*.[12] It was the best thing ever because I really got the whole thing around getting into people's worlds, building rapport, influencing, and directing them towards what needed to be achieved. It was great, really great. I remember an older Asian guy that I managed who could have been my uncle. There were times when he was almost dismissive when I asked him to help me do stuff in the store. And I was like, 'What's up with him?' There was a part of me that was afraid to confront it, so I didn't speak for a while. But another part of me said, 'Hold on a minute, this is my department and I need to show results. I need to show that the standards have been met. So I really do need to tackle this because I need this guy on my side.' So I had a respectful conversation with him. I got into his world and understood what was going on with him. It was brilliant. We sorted it out.

By the time I was 25, I was in senior management as an operations manager. I started to notice certain things in the business that we could do to improve, like listening to people and treating them better. Because, back in those days, managers could get away with shouting at staff on the shop floor. There was a lot more separation between management and staff. And it was just widely acceptable. Having seen this kind of behaviour on the shop floor, I vowed to do something about it. I had come up through the ranks, and I wanted to make a difference for people. The opportunity came when a director asked me, 'What do you really want to do?' That Friday, I was the operations manager, and, come Monday, I was the HR manager without experience or training.

My first placement as an HR manager was in an ethnically diverse East London store. When I first started the role, I observed how people were, what was going on for them, and what was important to them. There were quite a few Muslim staff members. During the month of Ramadan, I noticed that Muslim colleagues had no food available for when they broke their fast due to the canteen opening and closing times. They either had to bring in sandwiches or work

---

12 Dale Carnegie 'How to Win Friends and Influence People' Vermillion (2006)

on an empty stomach, as they had not eaten all day. So I organised, with the help of the canteen manager, to have hot food provided when they broke their fast. It was very well received. The Muslim staff felt valued. They felt like their needs were being met. That was when I understood that this was the right job for me.

Rather than sitting in the office, I started going into the shop and talking to people, getting to know them, asking them questions. I started finding out what was important to them, what they wanted and needed to feel valued. As I progressed, I moved to different stores and got recognised by my line managers for making a difference in some really tough shops. It was just awesome, and I thrived on it. I was helping the business to increase employee engagement and building managers' leadership skills. I was practicing what I'd read and used it to mentor others to get on in their careers. What was really great was having the opportunity to serve so many people.

When I moved to the head office for a while, we looked at how we could improve performance. One of my key roles was to create a policy and a training document to help managers conduct performance reviews. I remember writing, *'There's no such thing as poor performance, there's only disengagement. And disengagement is a result of poor leadership.'* Often managers say, *'We've got a number of staff who are not performing well.'* I disagree. It's not that they're under-performing—it's just that you haven't engaged them as a leader. There's something lacking in your leadership skills because when people are engaged, they do what needs to be done no matter what. I was in my 20s, and I was making these affirmations. On my journey around personal development, not only did I read *How to Win Friends and Influence People*, but closely after that, I read *The Seven Habits of Highly Effective* People,[13] which became my Bible. I practiced everything in that book and applied it at work, and found talent in the business. It was amazing.

I remember being at work in one of our shops and asking the young woman at the service desk to help me with all the Christmas display decorations. I asked her what she wanted to do in her career. She said, 'I want to develop myself and progress.' And I said, 'I can

---

13 Stephen R. Covey 'The Seven Habits of Highly Effective People', Simon & Schuster UK Ltd (1999)

help you do that, but you've got to be prepared to take on the feed-back and follow some simple things that I teach you to the letter. Then you will get to where you want to go.' There were times when I really pushed her because I had her back, and I knew she could do it. And she did it! Within seven months, she went from earning £16,000 a year to earning £28,000. She became the top-performing HR manager within the region. I supported her in her personal life by becoming her mentor. She was living in a studio flat at the time, and I encouraged her to put money aside and put a deposit down on a flat. She went on to smash it completely. She's now a landlord of three flats. She took on the mentoring and ran with it because she trusted me.

Claudia: So you identified talent in the business and guided them to take the essential steps that helped them progress. What essential steps did you take to get to where you are today?

Su: Although my work life was amazing, my home life throughout my childhood and into my teens was quite challenging. My mom came from India at the age of 16 and got married to my dad. She had me at 17 and, by the time she was 23, she had three children. She was young and didn't have a clue. My parents were factory workers who lived in rental accommodations and moved from rental to rental. I remember we rented a room for five of us in the landlord's house. I remember when I was about seven seeing the landlord's daughter in her own room, on her own big double bed. I was like, 'Why am I in a room with five people and she's got a room all to herself? When am I ever going to get that?' I remember her smacking me and bullying me because she felt territorial about her space. And I remembered telling my mom, expecting her to back me up, but she didn't because she couldn't do anything when we were living in the landlord's house. The thought that went into my mind was, 'Nobody's got my back.'

Throughout my life, I had loads of different experiences where I constantly felt like I wasn't backed up. My parents went to work, and I had nobody to talk to. At school, my friends would stop talking to me for no reason, and I had nobody but the dinner lady to talk to. All of these things contributed to my feeling that I wasn't good enough. So I ended up with very few friends because I was in a place where I couldn't trust people, and I felt better off being on my own. Then my parents got divorced when I was 14, which, in the 1980s for an Indian family, was scandalous and taboo. So that contributed further to my feeling unworthy.

I remember my mom struggling. She became a single parent with three kids and no support and no backup—nobody. Nothing. At college, I was very quiet and shy, with a complete lack of confidence and really low self-esteem. I was always thinking, 'I'm going to help my mom.' Going to uni would have meant being away from the family and not contributing, which is how I ended up at Tesco. Because I got this job at 16, I got used to earning and supporting my mom financially and in the house. So she'd go to work, and I'd cook dinner and have it ready for my brothers. I'd make sure they got home from school without glitches. I felt that I had to grow up really quickly, and I just started taking responsibility. I didn't want to let my mom down.

It was essential that I begin with the end in mind and set goals for my life, career, and finances. So, when I became a manager at Tesco at the age of 18, I started to visualise what I wanted for myself. Because of what I'd experienced in my family and my childhood, I wanted something completely different. One thing I wanted was to own my own house before I had kids. And I got my first house by the age of 26 despite obstacles along the way. I bought a second house by the age of 30, and I became a landlord. By the time I had my daughter, I had three properties, which is amazing, right? She had her own room decorated as she wanted it: My Little Pony, Peppa Pig, or whatever, and her own double bed. I was able to re-live my childhood through her by giving her that. And when she was born, I was able to work part-time because I'd created that financial security around me.

I qualified in HR whilst I was working full-time. So that was an essential step. I studied hard and paid for the course from my own pocket. I was determined to make something of my life; stand on my own two feet and be independent. I wanted to be financially secure so that when I had a child, I would be around for them and didn't have to work all the time. So I always set financial goals and achieved them. By the time I was 25, I was earning £25k, and by the time I was in my 30s, I was in a £50k job. And even at that very early age, I started learning about investing. I was really proud of the money I was earning, the investments I had built up, and the properties I owned.

I also set my career goals, which were probably my biggest goals. I would visualise myself at appraisal meetings every six months. I'd be like, 'What do I want my boss to be saying to me at that meeting?' And I would work towards that. I would see myself with my boss acknowledging me for achieving my targets and for making a difference. I would hear him saying, 'You know what, Su? You had an amazing year; you've achieved all of your targets.' Once I knew what my goal was, I always reverse-engineered and made sure I worked step by step towards it.

Another essential step was learning to influence people, and not just those in my team or department. It needs to be from the top down. I learned very early on that people need to feel important and valued. So I treated my team with the utmost respect. My bosses needed to feel good, too. I learned early on that you've got to build a relationship with your boss; that was more than him or her telling you what to do. It's about developing a relationship of what's going on with them. Asking, 'How are you?' 'What's going on with you?' 'What can I do to help you?' By doing this, your boss feels that their job is easier, and they buy into who you are as a person. I made sure my managers always knew that I had their back. To be successful, you have to win the hearts and minds of not just your team but your boss, too.

One of my managers transferred to another store and requested that I be his HR business partner because we made a great team and shared similar values. I've built great relationships with all my bosses. Even now, when I go to see clients, we talk business, but our relationship is very informal. They greet me with a hug rather than a handshake, and I'm involved in all their social events. It's great. They say, 'It's great to see you. I hope you're not going to end up leaving us because we want you to be part of our team.' It's important to help people at work to realise that it's ok to let your emotions show. We don't always have to be formal and robotic at work.

Claudia: Thanks for such great insight. Having led us through your essential steps towards transformation, what was the one most significant thing you did that got you into your current position?

Su: I've done many things. I've spent a lot of time on personal development, working on myself, and developing myself as a leader. I completed a leadership programme with Landmark Worldwide, and it transformed me to be the type of person I always wanted to be: to empower and lead others with love.

To be out there making a difference to others, you've got to take yourself on and deal with your inner demons. Those courses challenged me and transformed my life and how I perceived the world. For example, I hadn't spoken to my dad for about 15 years, and in my mind, I hated him really bad. He left us and hadn't contacted us, didn't speak to us on our birthdays. I constantly made him wrong, like, 'What kind of a dad doesn't care and doesn't want to make contact with his kids?' I made it all, 'I don't need my dad; he's dead as far as I'm concerned.' On the second day of the course, I realised that, actually, it didn't matter who my dad was for me; the real issue was who do I want to be for my dad? And when I got the realisation, I knew that I could choose to be however I wanted to be, and I didn't need to be so mad with him.

So I called him, and I was sobbing because I was just disgusted with myself and who I had become. He said, 'Why are you crying?' And I said, 'I feel really bad. I'm sorry. I haven't made an effort to be in your life.' And he said, 'Look, don't worry about it. How's my grand-daughter?' I found out that actually, my dad was just a very simple man. When he left us, he remarried and restarted his life. And that's how he has chosen to be. He's happy that he's got us in his life now. That year was the first year in I don't know how long my dad had me, my two brothers, my sisters-in-law, and all the grandkids around his house for his birthday.

I have created a life I want to live, who I want to be for other people, who I want to be for my daughter, and who I want to be for my health and my family. I always come back to being love, leadership, and empowerment for everyone.

Now I wake up every morning knowing that I'm going to make a difference to at least one person in the world. Sometimes it's really effortless like I'll post something on LinkedIn or on Facebook and people that I have never met before send me messages connecting with me saying things like, 'Your post has really inspired me,' or 'I've just gone and bought your book.' And it's so great to come across an HR professional who really cares about being human in the workplace. So it's transformed the way I am with people.

I'm role modelling all of this for my daughter. I want her to see that, no matter how hard things get, you can achieve anything you want. Having grown up with low self-esteem, I've made sure that everything I do with her is around encouraging her, developing her mindset, and listening to her. It's important to let kids make decisions from a young age. She makes most of the decisions about her life whilst I help her understand the consequences of her decisions so she can make informed choices.

Whenever confidence-building opportunities come up, I encourage her to grab them. She took part in her school's public speaking competition each year between the age of eight and 11, and she won. This led me to enrol her in Andy Harrington's public speaking course.

Claudia: For an Asian woman rising up the career ladder, Su, especially at such a young age, probably came with its fair share of challenges. What was the greatest challenge you faced on your journey? How did you overcome it?

Su: In February 2016, I left my second husband. In March the same year, I was made redundant, and in April, I had to sell my house. I lost my family network, job security, and my own home. I became a single parent, jobless, and lived in rented accommodation. My self-worth took a dive because I based it on the money I was earning, my job, the house I owned, the people I was around. Suddenly, I didn't own a house, and I didn't have a job. I didn't have people around me. I was on my own. I went through a state of real sadness and loneliness for a good few months. Maybe I was depressed. But luckily for me, my daughter had some exams coming up, and I had to stay strong for her. I couldn't let her see me being down and depressed. I had no choice but to be strong. We got through her 11-plus exams, and she was offered a place in the school she wanted.

Then I decided to get part-time work and went for a series of jobs and got none of them. I went through a stage of wondering why this crap kept happening in my life. I felt really overwhelmed and tired of being a strong woman. I started to think about giving up. But then I had a vision of myself being withdrawn, depressed, and lonely, staying in bed in my dressing gown with my greasy hair and not eating. And I saw my daughter coming home from the school concerned. 'Mom, have you eaten?' And I looked at this beautiful child and knew I couldn't do that to her. She deserved better.

I knew my mind wasn't in a great place, so I started listening to Tony Robbins' videos. They re-energised and inspired me, and I created a mindset plan. I developed a vision board and got my daughter to do one, too. I started working out and looking after my health and energy.

After I attended Andy Harrington's 'Power to Achieve' and went on to join his Professional Speakers Academy, I decided to set myself up in business. I created my own bespoke HR system, and now I train business owners and HR professionals. I built a plan around my business and where I wanted to go. Very soon, I got my first client, and I was on my way.

I don't think I've experienced challenges that are linked with my colour. But I've had challenges that were definitely related to my culture. My biggest challenge perhaps has been my relationship with money. I grew up in a very poor family from India. My parents came here and had nowhere to live. We rented rooms in other people's houses, and life was about thriving and surviving. I had uniform vouchers for my school clothes and free school meals. That was the level we were at. I had no idea as a child what it might feel like to have money.

My relationship with money has always been very poor because we never had much, I guess. Whilst growing up, we were always encouraged not to waste money or spend money on certain things. The message I was given about money was that you didn't need to be rich—you just needed to have enough money.

I picked up all these stories from my culture and my parents' beliefs about money when I was younger. And I'd hear from other people around me, but not from my parents, that rich people are snobby, arrogant, or whatever. Even on birthdays when relatives gave us money as a gift, my parents were like, 'No, don't take the money,' as if it's a really bad thing to take other people's money in that way. Pretty much everyone in my family is dealing with that challenge. They don't dream big because maybe they don't have that sense of self-worth. In India, you're not encouraged to dream big; you're not encouraged to be someone who can go out there and make things happen, whether you're a man or a woman. You might think, 'It would be great to be a millionaire, but that's not meant for me.'

So my relationship with money has been a big challenge in my business because I really hold back from asking people for it. I've been listening to this amazing book called *Happy Money* by a guy named Ken Honda. He talks about money IQ, which is about how to make money. And then he talks about money issues, which is about your feelings about money. He says that often what we create for ourselves when we're paying bills or our taxes, for example, is this fear at the back of our mind about not ever getting that money back. So when we give the money out, it's attached to fear, and we're coming from a place of lack and scarcity. And that's what I've been doing pretty much most of my life.

I've really had to fight my old beliefs around money and being wealthy and all of that kind of stuff. But I've decided that I don't want to be like that anymore. I've looked at those limiting beliefs, and asked myself, 'What is the truth?' I have a completely different mindset now. I'm aiming to be different, to go out there in the world and publish a book, be a keynote speaker, things my family are so proud of.

My generation of Indians is bringing up their children with completely different attitudes. My daughter won speaker of the year in 2018. So she's been encouraged to speak up and speak out. There's no dumbing down or shutting up. She has a completely different lifestyle compared to when I was growing up. I have given her the opportunity to experience money from a very young age. She has her vision board of what she wants in her life and how she wants it to be. So she's already dreaming on that level. I think lots of Indian parents from the generation before me have experienced that hardship, and they have really pushed their kids to study hard and aim higher.

Although, in some parts of India, boys and men are valued more than girls and women, that was never the case in my world. As the oldest child in my family, I've always been very strong-minded because my strong-minded mom was my role model. She would do anything for anyone. She would make life work, despite being a single parent from her early 30s when she and my dad split up.

I just started going out there and making things happen rather than crumbling and feeling sorry for myself. I remember when I worked for Tesco, and I was kind of developing in my roles. I would see lots of male-duty managers in the store. I remember going up to my store managers and saying, 'Why can't I be a duty manager? If he can do it, I can do it.' I was lucky because I worked in a company that had lots of opportunities. It was there if you wanted it.

The only time I experienced difficulty as a female in my culture was in my first marriage. Oh my God, it was horrendous! I had been dating this guy for about a year, and we got married. I'd been to his house, and I knew that we would be living with his family; his mom, particularly, but he never showed me the side of him that he became. On our honeymoon, I found out that he was a control freak. And, during the marriage, he wanted a maid in the house for his mom. I remember sitting in the living room one day, and he said, 'Go and ask my mom if she wants a cup of coffee.' And I'm like, 'Why don't you go and ask her?' When visitors or family came over, his mom was like, 'Your place is in the kitchen.' So I experienced that domination in my marriage, which I wouldn't have minded doing had it not been a matter of 'that's the way things are.' Although I tried to make it work for a couple of years, I shared with them that I wasn't happy, but nobody listened. Needless to say, it didn't last long.

I was a senior manager at Tesco at the time. I was making big decisions at work, and I would go home and be like a mouse. I didn't go through all the challenges I'd gone through and develop my career, and I didn't see my mom go through all the challenges she had gone through to then live my life like a doormat. I was certain that that wasn't what I was made to do. So I legged it, and I never looked back.

Claudia: With all the challenges you've had to overcome and everything you've achieved, I'm guessing that you probably had a big moment of insight somewhere along the way. What was it?

Su: I discovered the power of sharing my message on social media. I posted a video on Facebook about connecting with Dad after 15 years. The message impacted many people, and they reached out to let me know how they reconnected with their parents after watching my video. So I started sharing a lot more which, in turn, improved my confidence. My Facebook community helped me to feel more connected and less isolated. I have also achieved amazing results in my business.

I wrote my book, and I share it on LinkedIn regularly. We all want the freedom to be self-expressed and limitless, and we are all dealing with our conditioning.

Claudia: Congratulations on the success of your book, Su. What resources have been crucial to your overall success?

Su: I am very self-aware and have become resourceful at managing my mindset. I recognise when my mindset isn't in a good place, and I need to do something. So I'm proactive and plug myself into motivational YouTube videos, books, meditation, or call one of my peers. I feel so blessed to have people around me that have my back.

The community of people I have created and surrounded myself with are very important. These are people who help you remember your greatness, who you truly are, which is important because there are days when you can't see how good you are and all you've achieved. Sometimes you need people you trust to wake you up during such incredibly dark times; people who've got your back, people who won't let you fail and who want you to succeed—sometimes more than you might want to. I have been fortunate to work with some amazing coaches and mentors who have had my back.

Claudia: Doing what you do for HR departments involves leadership, I would say. What's your understanding of leadership?

Su: Leadership is about you as a leader developing yourself to 'Be the change you want to see in others', and listening to others as leaders. Everyone out there is a leader; they just need help with seeing it.

My coaching now is about empowering others to be self-led. I encourage people to get connected to who they are first—their true selves—and then to go out there and lead others.

Claudia: How has that understanding of leadership informed your role as a woman of colour and a leader?

Su: Leadership is about serving others, and I advocate inclusion. It shouldn't matter what gender, colour, or creed people come from. In my model of the world, there's no difference. There's no creed, there's no colour, and there's no gender. For me, the opportunities are out there for everybody. It's all about how you develop your mindset to respond to different situations. You know, I have not ever experienced any form of inequality. I can go out there and speak on stage as well as any man. I know my limitations, but they're not because I'm a woman, or because I'm Indian, or because I'm 5 feet tall. It's got nothing to do with that. If something isn't working, it's because I haven't quite developed that space in my mind, rather than the circumstances or other people. I have learnt that life is an inside-out job!

Claudia: So what you are saying is that success as a leader is about mindset and how you respond to challenges. Bearing this in mind, what are your top three tips for women who want to be leaders in their field?

Su: First, get to know who you are. What is your purpose? Your values? Who are you? And be really grounded in that. Knowing that love, leadership, and empowerment are my key values, I can bring these to anything in my life. Because when you don't know who you are, you will try to fit into what other people are and what they want. And you get confused; you're not living with integrity or according to your own values, which doesn't work. You'll feel friction in your personality and your relationships with other people.

It's so important to be grounded in who you are. I know that wherever I go and whoever I'm with, I'm love, leadership, and empowerment. That's who I am for other people, for myself, for my family, and for my world. So anything that goes against that I stay away from. When you know who you are, you can live authentically, and life just works out fine.

I'm a woman of colour, but I don't differentiate myself in that way. I do so according to who I am as a human being. Because I believe that, when we start thinking about women of colour or women, men, gender, or whatever, we begin to create division. I live my life being very inclusive. So I don't see myself as being an Indian woman. In the world out there, I see myself as a woman or a leader who empowers people, whether you're a man or a woman, Indian, black or white—it doesn't matter. It's all about how can I empower, lead, and be a symbol of love for other people. I separated from my husband in 2016, and we are like best friends now. We co-parent my daughter. My mother-in-law still makes dinner for us sometimes. So, we're still a family, which is really awesome. So it's just creating who you need to BE as a human being.

Second, make your life about serving others and causing an impact in the world. As a child, I felt disempowered and disconnected, and now, by serving and empowering others, I have love around me in abundance.

Third, develop healthy proactive self-care habits, and be disciplined enough to practice them every day. Don't underestimate the power of affirmations, meditation, exercise, gratitude journaling, and visualisation. Create balance in your day, and give energy to all areas of the wheel of life—daily.

'I knew I could get promoted like the guys. My bosses saw me using my initiative, taking risks, and helping the business. So they supported me, and I developed my leadership skills. When I was 18, I was promoted and began managing older and more experienced colleagues.'

— Su

CHAPTER 5

Dr Jacqueline: The Mental Health Charity Founder and Director

Few people know that suicide is one of the leading causes of death in children and young people in the UK.[14] Considering that one in six children aged 5 -16 is likely to have a mental health issue, you'd be forgiven for believing that appropriate intervention would be obtainable at a sufficiently early age. However, 75 per cent of children and young people experiencing mental health problems don't get the intervention they need, whilst 34 per cent of those referred to NHS services are not accepted into treatment.[15] Shocking, right?

My Page 1 Woman is determined to turn this around. She's Dr. Jacqueline Campbell (aka Jax). She was knocked off course when her younger brother took his own life. Setting up the Julian Campbell Foundation with a vision to enable children and young people to manage their mental health is her own way of ensuring that her brother, Julian, did not die in vain. She said young people are *under-represented in terms of support provision. Statistics show that 50 percent of mental health conditions (e.g. bulimia, depression, or anxiety) are experienced by the age of 14. And it takes 10 years, on average, before they get support. So many young people fall through the net. And then they become adults, and, for example, they face a crisis such as losing a loved one and they have to be sectioned. We want to prepare them to manage these events so that their mental health and well-being aren't seriously affected.'

---

14 Royal College of Paediatrics and Child Health (2020) State of Child Health. London: RCPCH. [Available at: stateofchildhealth.rcpch.ac.uk]

15 The Children's Society https://www.childrenssociety.org.uk/what-we-do/our-work/well-being/mental-health-statistics.

So, who is Dr. Jacqueline Campbell? She is a recipient of the Mental Health Foundation's Black Innovators in Mental Health award (2020), alongside the likes of Archbishop Desmond Tutu. She is tenacious, enthusiastic, purpose-driven, and unstoppable. As a former teacher who had climbed the ladder into teaching consultancy, she has a dogged ambition to ensure that her brother's death was not in vain, that something beyond good comes out of his tragic passing, and that children and young people with mental health issues get the support and help they deserve.

The Foundation is not just a memorial to Julian's name; it's a provision that Jax is determined to make a permanent fixture in schools countrywide. The impact of the global COVID-19 pandemic on the mental health of children and young people has shone a welcome light on how significantly the service offered by this kind of charity is needed.

Keep reading to find out more about the Julian Campbell Foundation and its founder, Dr. Jacqueline Campbell.

THE INTERVIEW

Claudia: Describe what you do, Jax.

Jax: I'm the founder of the Julian Campbell Foundation, a registered charity that empowers young people to manage their mental health. The organisation is named to honour my brother, Julian, who took his own life in 2007 due to long-standing struggles with his mental health.

At first, after Julian died, I was paralyzed with grief. I didn't know what to do. I began setting up the charity around 2010 when I was still in the teaching profession. Then, in 2011, my own M.E. condition forced me to examine what in my life was really important. I chose to give up teaching and do the charity work whilst caring for my mom. I'd already had a 20-year career as a science teacher and then as a consultant going into challenging schools to raise teaching and learning standards.

The Foundation helps young people, aged 11 to 24, identify how they're feeling and shows them how to change their mood to avoid becoming stressed out and anxious about the things that really matter and get to them—things like exams, bullying, family breakups, and new family structures. We help them develop their emotional intelligence so they will be able to consider the impact of their behaviour on others. We run drama workshops in schools, which is a fun way of showing a young person how to identify and manage their well-being. We also mentor those who need specific support and guidance. In addition, we train teachers to recognise signs of mental health problems so that they can take early action.

We also offer a befriending service to parents of children who have taken their own lives. I see these parents once a week and allow them to empty themselves of their emotions by talking about their child and sharing their pictures. Obviously, it's a really difficult time for them because losing a child is the worst thing that could ever happen to any parent. They don't expect their child to die before them or take their own life. Seeing my parents go through the loss of their son was dreadful. I had to organise my brother's funeral, as my parents had just completely lost it. So I saw this need for support for bereaved parents. It's not easy, but it's something I like doing.

It sounds bizarre to say that I like doing it, but it's really fulfilling to support these parents living through such a hard condition and hearing about their children. Most people don't know how to be with such overwhelming grief or how to respond to them. Most people just don't know what to say and probably worry about saying the wrong things. But I sit and listen and help them to talk.

Julian was handsome, gifted, kind-hearted, intelligent, talented, and with so much potential. And yet, it happened. The two of us had some interesting and unique conversations. When he died, I sought out the things that could have made a difference in his life. I found that there was not much in place. I looked back to when he was a teenager and in school. When I was involved in staff training in the schools where I worked, there was training about special needs and managing children with autism, or Asperger's. But there was absolutely nothing about managing children experiencing stress, anxiety, and depression. I went to many schools, and, you know, it was always the same thing.

At the start of 2020, we were a medium-sized charity that got a lot done for the money. However, the COVID-19 pandemic led to a rapid expansion, and we found ourselves operating in an international market. The impact of the pandemic and lockdown on the mental health of children and young people sent parents and teachers in search of the kind of support the Foundation provides. Early in 2020, we had the capacity to support up to 50 children and young people. Now we are supporting 300 at a time. We've gone from 10 volunteer mentors and 10 drama facilitators to 30 and 16, respectively. We also have three directors (one of which is me), and we have psychologists and trustees who hold me accountable and provide me with tremendous support. I manage the finances. I could never have predicted that a nasty global pandemic that has wreaked havoc in so many different countries would have given the charity the opportunity to reach so many children and young people and create a waiting list of schools and parents wanting our services.

I do a lot of speaking engagements about our research on young people and mental health issues. I also arrange a lot of fundraising activities like sponsored runs and skydiving done by people who contact us and are willing to help. That's how we generate our main income to move things forward.

Claudia: Moving from teaching to helping youngsters with mental health issues couldn't have been easy. What essential steps got you to where you are currently?

Jax: Realising my passion for mental wellness and giving up my career was absolutely essential. The charity would not have been set up without those events. In the beginning, I was still working as a teacher, looking after my mom, and running the charity. I was using my salary to support it. Then I stopped enjoying teaching. Becoming a head teacher has never been part of my career plan because promotion takes you away from the kids, and I loved teaching young people and being in their space. But I became more and more tired, more and more worn out. Obviously, I was doing too much. And then one day, I just couldn't get out of bed.

For eight or nine months, I was in that same space, not knowing what to do. I'd go to an interview, get the job, and I wouldn't last the first day because I was already exhausted and lacked energy. I realised that something had to change. The teaching had to stop. I had to focus on what was most important to me—my mom and the charity. I gave up a really good salary, and didn't know how to claim an employment support allowance, as I'd been working for 20-odd years. One minute I was earning a comfortable salary, and the next, I was getting very little income. It was shocking.

Unlike teaching, I can now work my own hours and do as much as I want. During that period when I was really tired, it would take all day to write a text, but I did not give up because I had this desire to carry on regardless, make a difference in children's and young people's lives, and get the wellness agenda out there into the wider world.

Another essential step was when I was doing my brother's eulogy at the funeral. At that moment, I decided to do something in his name. But I didn't know what. Three years later, after the worst of my grieving was over, I got the idea to combine my teaching experience and knowledge of secondary schools and I created a vision for the charity. And that's how it all started. I now have some awesome people involved who share my vision. It's really humbling.

Our referrals come to us through schools and, since the pandemic, via the internet. With COVID-19, we obviously can't go into schools the same way, and we now work with children and young people online. I've found that as time has gone on, our clients if you can call them that, have gotten younger and younger. We're seeing kids experiencing panic attacks, eating disorders, or self-harm. The younger they come to us, the quicker we can make an impact and turn things around. So, for that reason, I'm happy. But supporting those at the top-end of our age group is harder because, chances are, their experiences of mental health issues have been going on for a while. So it's harder to effect change.

Claudia: You've just told us about the essential steps that moved you forward. But was there a one really significant thing that helped, too? If so, what was it?

Jax: I remember watching Steven Fry's three-part documentary about bipolar (Julian's condition). At the end of part two, he was speaking to the inspirational Dr. Liz Miller, a top neurosurgeon, about her experience of being diagnosed with bipolar and being sectioned. She's written a book about it, parts of which I've gone on to integrate into our mentoring and teacher training programmes. Dr. Liz Miller is now one of our trustees.

I also wrote a book in 2018, *Runs in the Family*, about how I got here—founding a charity, the difficulties both my brother and I faced, the work we do, and how we support young people. The book is mainly for young parents because I've seen the troubles young people and their families pass through. Often, we mentor the young person and their parents, too, as it moves things on more quickly. And then, I saw that supporting parents earlier could prevent the difficulties their children experience. So the book is to show young parents how to look at themselves, manage their own mental health, and prepare efficiently well for parenthood.

Another significant thing was that I was invited onto Sky's Ben TV in the summer of 2019. I was in Columbia that year when somebody invited me to speak about the charity. I thought, 'I'm in

Columbia; can I really afford the time and the expenditure?' But then I saw the opportunity and, interestingly, it was around the time of Julian's birthday. I had to book three flights to get there, and I was so jetlagged when I arrived. But I was really pleased about it. I got a lot of exposure and a 20-minute video of me talking about the charity, which I can use for marketing purposes. I was invited to come back to the show at any time. It was a really good experience talking about the charity on TV. But also, through it, we attracted new ambassadors, such as Glenn McCauley, the former heavyweight boxing champion, and a 12-year-old boy on 'Tea Talk.'

Claudia: Leading in teaching and setting up a charity like yours must have been demanding for you as a black woman. What was your greatest challenge, and how did you overcome it?

Jax: As a science teacher, I've had people copying my stuff, passing it off as theirs, and not giving me credit. I've faced the usual stereotypes about black women—we can't possibly be science teachers; we aren't smart enough. We can only be entertainers in the performing arts department.

When I was doing my PhD, I was doing something I really enjoyed that inspired me and that was going to help raise standards in the classroom. But I experienced lots of barriers, although in those days, I wasn't very aware of racism. So I couldn't see the discrimination that was taking place, although my mom could see it clearly and would often point it out. I came across some jealous people, which may or may not be due to race.

When I was Head of Department, it was difficult because I would ask people to do things, and they wouldn't do it. At one school, where I just happened to have been a pupil and returned as Head of Department, my old chemistry teacher was still there. He didn't seem to like that I was his manager. Sometimes my staff meetings were a joke because of the way he responded to me and undermined me in front of everyone.

Not being taken seriously was really stressful and upsetting. I kept a lot of it to myself. I didn't want to speak about it. I didn't want it to dominate, as there was a lot going on in the school at the time.

It was really hard. These were all people that maybe weren't used to having a black woman manager. I later found out that I was the first black woman senior teacher at that school. But I don't see things that way. Because for me, it's more about focusing on my job rather than on myself; about raising standards and helping more kids get better grades because that was their passport. Perhaps I could have still done my job and be savvy about the barriers that people were putting up against me. But I didn't want to go down that road because I didn't know if I would come out of it. I might have got stuck in there, bitter and blaming and acting irresponsibly.

I have always had my strategies. In a school setting, I was pretty much unstoppable because I made a point of learning from every job I had. I evaluated what I was doing and where I could have gone wrong. There was one point where I didn't speak up quickly enough and got into trouble. Well, I decided in my next job that I would point out what wasn't working more quickly. In the school setting, people were often surprised when they saw the increase in my pupils' science grades. So they started giving me every underperforming year group, which meant that they kept the best groups for themselves. Noticing this, I changed the timetable so that the underperforming year groups were shared equally.

The greatest challenge in the charity has been to keep going. When you're in teaching, things are more certain. You know students will gain certain qualifications, and you know how things will eventually go. But in a charity, it's always uncertain. You always have funding in mind and how to raise it.

I often reach out to other charities because I think it's good to share and collaborate. I remember contacting the CEO of a very big charity, and the meeting didn't end so well. I don't know if there was some professional jealousy there, although mine is just a little charity, but he wanted to see my CV. It didn't cross my mind that it was to do with me being a black woman. That CEO was also a black man, but he was asking to see my CV. One of my trustees spotted what was happening and said, 'That's out of order.' But at the time, I just did not see it like that. We've also faced a lot of resistance from established charities in the mental health field. I'm not sure why. But it has been so frustrating.

I have moved from being someone with consultant status in teaching, a great reputation which got me headhunted to turn schools around, to being a 'nobody' working in the mental health field. So it was really, really hard to keep going sometimes. I had a proven track record in education but no track record in mental health. So I don't know if it was about my credibility or if I was seen as a potential threat. I don't understand why I had so much opposition. Why wasn't I embraced? Why no 'There are lots of kids that you can help; why don't you come to this or that meeting?' Or there were empty promises when we contacted schools directly, and we were invited in. We would then train our mentors to support identified young people, but those schools didn't invite us back.

I didn't push my previous achievements—all my awards and reputation—because I thought they were unrelated. I even dropped my doctor title. It may have all been due to getting chronic fatigue syndrome, which made me feel like a failure. I realised that I'd been pushing myself to go after the next qualification or the next accomplishment to prove myself. Since having M.E. and then turning my life around, I'm no longer after that verification. My religion and all those mentors I've had in my life have taught me to be gentle with myself.

Claudia: With all those challenges, how do you keep yourself going?

Jax: I keep myself going because I don't want my brother to have died for no reason. I want something good to come out of his death. And if the good is that all the schools in our country have courses that help and support young people to manage their mental health and well-being, then I'll know my job is done. I can't stop anyway, even though sometimes I think, 'Why have I been chosen to do this? Why can't somebody else do this?' Or 'There are a lot of other people doing it.' Sometimes I have anxiety attacks. But something drives me, and it's hard to explain exactly what that is. Maybe it's my brother's constant memory. Training for fundraising runs when I'm stressed and feeling negative makes me feel more positive.

Claudia: When you have a real purpose, like you, and you're facing tough challenges, I guess they'll trigger lightbulb moments. What was your greatest lightbulb moment?

Jax: My greatest lightbulb moment was realising that if I can get people like Tito Jackson (Michael Jackson's brother) involved in the organisation, I can encourage more celebrities to do so, too. We've a plan to get more celebrity endorsements. I got the idea when I was inspired by a flash mob on 'Britain's Got Talent', who were also world dance champions. I got them to perform at Kings Cross on World Mental Health Day, 10 October 2017. Then I contacted other celebrities. The response was varied. Many celebrities were interested but not interested enough.

Another important lightbulb moment came as a result of our recent expansion. It made me realise that face-to-face mentoring was not the only way to work and is actually quite limited. I realised that mentoring children and young people and running drama workshops online would help us to reach so many more and is a lot more efficient. And that's what we have done.

I also recognised that all the hard work and my ridiculously long workdays, the challenges we had experienced as a charity, and our slow rate of growth were all preparing us for this moment. The pandemic struck, and as a result, so many people need what we are offering.

Claudia: To have a successful teaching career, then set up a charity and keep it going, you'll need some significant resources. What resource has been crucial to your success?

Jax: The greatest resource was getting a PhD. My PhD in cognitive psychology and raising intelligence in young people enabled me to go into schools as a consultant. It boosted my confidence and helped me get promoted more rapidly into the leadership team.

Now it's helping me in my current role. I'm writing a research report from a public health perspective using the same PhD research techniques and methodology. So I'm well equipped. I've also got two Masters: one in education and the other in public health because I wanted to have knowledge of managing health in populations.

As a black woman, I very much doubt that I would be where I am today had I not been so well-educated. All that studying and all my qualifications have helped me to get short-listed and then interviewed for every job I've gone for. I didn't really have to work too hard to get my positions. So I think that without my qualifications it wouldn't have been the same.

But interestingly, when I was still in teaching, it was difficult to use my PhD title of doctor. I thought it was easier not to use it because it comes with its own complications. In my experience, it was better that people didn't know I had a doctorate. There was one school I went to where it was always a topic of discussion in the classrooms. And sometimes, it just seemed like people really had it in for me. They didn't like me having that title. I just thought to myself, 'Well, this only started when I got this title,' so then I stopped using it, and I just had a quieter life, which is what I wanted. It may have been due to professional jealousy, I don't know. It may have been due to me being a black woman with a prestigious title. I guess I'll never know for sure.

Now I'm running this charity. I can see that it gives me a lot more credibility, but it's taken me a while to pluck up the courage to use it after my experience in education.

Claudia: As a former leader in schools and now a leader in a charity, what do you understand by leadership?

Jax: Leadership is being a visionary; having a goal, so you know where you're taking everybody. You need to be able to manage that and take account of your followers' needs. Leaders aren't always appointed. You can lead by initiating action and influencing others even though you may not have the title of leader.

As a woman leader, other people provide a mirror for me. I see aspects of myself that work or don't work through what's happening around me. I'm not sure if that's about being a woman. Maybe because I'm a woman, I'm more compassionate.

My style is more of a democratic kind—involving everyone, giving them a say—because it's their organisation. Maybe men are more autocratic. I'm not sure. As a woman, I operate with integrity, and I want to make a difference in young people's lives. But that might be true for men, too.

Claudia: So what difference has it made being a black woman leader?

Jax: I think that all of my training and skills, being a teacher, being a manager, being my brother's carer, and the carer of my mom and dad, have contributed to forging me into who I am. And the skills that I have in management and dealing with people have mainly been learned from the teams that I led when I was a teacher. You can have all of the ideas and be a visionary, but if you don't know how to manage people, it can be quite difficult. Each person is complicated and different.

What I find difficult is that we've had to recruit a lot of volunteers, as we haven't got a big budget. And so, my thing is how do I keep volunteers coming back because we haven't got money to pay them? So I have to be the best version of myself and make sure that we are mentoring and supporting them and helping them achieve their dreams and goals. I might not be able to give them money, but I can give them an incredible and worthwhile experience.

All of those things have been so because of how I've been brought up as a black girl and what I've learned along the way. You know, I've learned that it's not all about money. I used to think that once we had money, we could pay people, and we'd get a better service. But it's not that at all. People want a good experience, as it makes them feel good. I guess they want to know that they're making a real difference with what they're doing as well.

I've also learned that despite the challenges and setbacks, despite people doubting my abilities and what I could achieve as a black girl and then as a woman, despite my former tutor telling me I was incompetent, I can achieve whatever I want if I set my mind to it and if I'm determined and never give up. And actually, I've done exactly that and have proved them all wrong. That's all about me being a black woman.

In my darkest moments, when I feel that I've had enough and I'm tired, it's my passion for making a difference that sees me through. I'm not saying men don't have that, but that's just about me as Jax, the black woman. That's what it is. Maybe it is that caring element, caring for the families, caring for the children and young people. Providing mentors for young people and for parents as well because that speeds up the rate of improvement; gives it more velocity. You know, I don't want that family to be as dysfunctional as mine was sometimes, with my brother having arguments with my dad, and I'm trying to keep the peace. I want those families to have some peace.

Claudia: So, what are your top three tips for women of colour who want to be leaders in their field?

Jax: Have a vision and purpose. Once you know what you want and why then the rest falls into place. When you know that you're filling a gap and making a difference, you've got direction—you're unstoppable, confident, and driven. You're forced to take action. And on those days where things are going badly, that vision and purpose will still find a way to drive you. Through losing my brother, I discovered my 'why'. And knowing that I'm making a difference is satisfying.

I used to be a real party animal and a clubber who was out every night having fun. And then my brother died, and I became so confused. I just didn't know what my purpose was or why I was here. Many of us don't take the time to find out what we're here for. I strongly believe the reason why I'm here now is because of what happened to my brother. My purpose is to set up this charity and help children and young people with their mental health. And maybe I'm here to ensure that children and young people of colour don't get left out. Who knows? Knowing my purpose is so satisfying. It makes my life worthwhile because I know I'm making a difference to those families. And I know we're helping those young people to succeed in whatever field they have chosen.

Second, find your passion. When you find your purpose, you'll find your passion. They're intertwined. It comes through listening to yourself and finding out what you really want and need. It brings you alive and gets you focused and driven. You'll get what you want with velocity. As women of colour, things can get really tough because of discrimination and racism. And when they do get difficult, your passion will keep you focused and get you through. That's what I've always found. My passion for what I do has kept me going through all the pain, sadness, and challenges I've gone through.

It's just so easy for us to get lost in the overwhelming distractions of the world and never find ourselves. Some people go through their whole lives like that. It requires you to take time out for yourself to think. For me, it was unusual to do that because I was so used to being on the hamster treadmill. I was a teacher planning the year ahead. I had my calendar, my year-at-a-glance, and all the meetings. Then I had my personal life alongside all of that. So I wasn't really able to think for myself and identify what I needed. And then I started stepping back from all of that madness and my teaching and my career. I started thinking about what it was I really wanted and what I was passionate about. When my brother died, after the grieving period, things started falling into place, So it's really listening to yourself and identifying your passion and what you want and need.

Third, believe in yourself. And when people come with their agenda and try to change what you want and what you have created, you'll stay firm about what you want. Self-belief provides strength and solid conviction that you're doing the right thing. Otherwise, you're all over the place, going down other people's routes. And maybe years later, you realise you're out there, lost, in the middle of nowhere.

Believing in yourself and having that conviction that you can do it, regardless of what people say or do, gets you to where you want to go much more quickly. It helps you break through those many obstacles that we, as women of colour face. It makes you unstoppable. So when you feel like giving up, just remember who you are, what you're capable of, and what you've already pulled off. You'll stay the course.

'I keep myself going because I don't want my brother to have died for no reason. I want something good to come out of his death. And if the good is that all the schools in our country have courses that help and support young people to manage their mental health and well-being, then I'll know my job is done.'

— Jax

CHAPTER 6

Michelle: The Book Mentor and Publisher

I often stand on the platform of a London underground tube line and wonder who might be staring at me from the darkest depths of the driver's cabin. As a product of Western socialisation, I have to own up to imagining that it's a bloke. Well, stereotypically, train driving is viewed as a man's job, right?

When Hannah Dadds made history in 1978 by becoming the first woman to drive a London underground train, she was paving the way for change in an industry traditionally reserved for men. But was she aware that that single mould-breaking act would inspire so many women that, 43 years later, 100 or more of us are tube train drivers? This particular Page 1 Woman used to be one of them. Involving 15 weeks of gruelling training and exams, it's definitely not a career anyone can easily walk into.

'I really feel good about having been a tube train driver because it's not an easy job to get. It's more than just pushing buttons. You have to learn so much about the train and how the system works.'

Let me introduce you to Michelle Watson. She gave up driving trains to become an author, a charismatic speaker, and a book writing and business acceleration coach. She's a mom of three to boot. Michelle is an everyday woman who has experienced incredibly dark times, during which she hid her true self from the world and was driven to the brink of utter despair. But her newfound religious faith was pivotal in wheeling her life around and cultivating her peace of mind. Sharing her experience in her first book was the catalyst that propelled her into coaching. Now, with her purpose seemingly clear, she's on a journey to something bigger and brighter that makes a real difference in people's lives.

Incredibly warm, charismatic, courageous, ambitious, and possessing a wicked and winning sense of humour, here's Michelle in her own words.

THE INTERVIEW

Claudia: So, Michelle, share with us what you do.

Michelle: I am a book mentor and publisher, the founder of Breakfree Forever Consultancy Ltd. I serve entrepreneurs, speakers, business start-ups, and individuals who want to share their stories and expertise with the world so as to make an impact, create income, increase their business, and leave a profound legacy behind.

My first book was written for people going through challenges, such as parenting children with special needs like my son, perhaps domestic abuse, or even suicidal tendencies, both of which I have experienced on a personal level. Basically, the book highlights challenges within the home and examines them from an outsider's viewpoint. People peering in from the outside don't really understand what you're going through, and that was the main reason why I wrote the book. People see you and they think, 'Her life is great. It's all good.' Or they may be very judgemental of your child's behaviour because they don't know what's really going on. I thought, 'Why not write this book and make people aware?' But, at first, I hesitated. I didn't think anyone would read it. Then one day, a colleague with a dysfunctional child broke down at work. I gave her some useful information and shared the story about my son having ADHD and traits of autism. It cheered her up. That incident prompted me to write the book. It's called, *Overcome and Rise Above: How to Turn the Downsides of Your Challenges into the Upside of Renewing Your Life.* The book also covers my experience of domestic abuse in my first marriage and my attempt to take my own life.

My second book, *Rise Above and Believe—It's Do or Lie: How to Get Rid of Excuses & Create the Life You Desire*, is for procrastinators with dreams who set goals but find excuses for never following them through only because they don't believe in themselves enough. That's why 'It's Do or Lie', because sometimes our excuses are actually lies—reasons to avoid doing something, or maybe as a result of self-limiting beliefs or the circle of influence we are in, or plainly just not knowing what right steps to take.

It's based on my experience. After I came out of that abusive relationship, I had low self-esteem, although people wouldn't have noticed it because I'm always jovial. I was busy rushing around, but come year-end, I had nothing substantial to show for it. I didn't believe I could finish what I'd started because I didn't believe I had the capability.

This same thing happens to other people. They say they are taking action, but for me, if your action doesn't produce results, then you've not taken any action at all. I really woke up when I got into the personal development world and learned Neuro-Linguistic Programming and all that stuff. I realised that I'd not really been taking action. Truth be told, I was doing stuff, but it was centred on other people's dreams and their benefit. So I had to address that, which was the purpose of my second book.

My third book came out in January 2020, and it's called *Authority: How to Write a Business Book and Use It as a Marketing Tool*. It does exactly what it says on the tin. As a book writing coach, my market is small business owners, entrepreneurs, and young women who are looking for ways to get their story out there and build a business behind it. Some people have a powerful story related to their passion and business or the business they aim to have. They want to share that story, but they just don't know how to go about it, how to start gaining visibility, or even where to start.

Having been successful with my first two books, I was mentoring budding authors for a book company. What I came to realise was that a lot of people were paying five figures for book coaching, and yet, after two years or more, they still didn't have a book or a business. They were just left to their own devices. Some people were paying out the last of their savings and were expecting big financial returns, right? And they didn't get it. Having once been in debt and having once made wrong financial choices, I felt for those people because I didn't want them to reach that point where they had invested the last of their savings into a programme that promised them a successful business and gave them little or none.

It didn't sit well with me because people spending that amount of money should get at least some sort of follow-up, some sort of coaching, some sort of guidance on the way. I thought to myself, 'Well, what if I could create something that would help the people that cannot afford to pay five figures? What if I could give them a great book writing experience? I can actually help somebody else to do that and not have them go bankrupt in doing so.' The thing is, a lot of people can start a journey or go to all these seminars where they are told, 'Yeah, you can do it.' They get all pumped up. But then, when they go back home, and they're on their own, they're surprisingly stuck. So I wanted to help those people that wanted to have a voice, those people that had a powerful story to tell, to get it out there without being ripped off. At the same time, I wanted to help them turn their ideas into something more because that was my experience. And I thought, 'I wanted to be that middle person as well as being a coach and mentor in Breakfree Forever Consultancy.' I have my own publishing company, Breakfree Forever Publishing. My books are all available on Amazon.

Claudia: What made you swop the exciting world of driving tube trains for book mentoring and publishing?

Well, I gave up driving trains in 2019 because, although it was exhilarating, it was not my purpose. I'm now on a mission to change lives. It is funny really because, as a train driver, I was taking people from destination A to destination B, and that exactly is my passion but in a different form. My mission is to help individuals by showing them how to get from the stage they are in their lives right now (Point A) to where it is that they desire to be (Point B).

I was in banking before I became a train driver. I never envisioned myself driving trains, but when my friend suggested I apply, I realised that I could earn as much doing it part-time as I was getting working full-time in the bank. Also, it allowed me ample time to work around my son. At the time, I was always being called by the school to pick him up, so I needed time to work around his needs. And it gave me the space and money to create my own business and achieve my purpose. In fact, a lot of my ideas for my book got downloaded to me whilst I was driving the train.

I enjoyed people's reactions when I said that I drove trains. They were amazed. They were like, 'What? Wow! That's something for a woman to do being a train driver!' They just didn't expect it. It made me feel good because, to be honest, studying to become a train driver was hard, and I made it.

I used to enjoy being alone in the dark cab, where I got my me-time and space and business ideas. I used to start at 4 a.m. and finish at mid-day, and then it was home, followed by the school run and having to be there for my children after school. So I didn't really get much time for myself. So being alone in the darkness of the driver's cab was important. Now I work part-time in an office instead of driving trains, and I run my business alongside it, and I'm a mum of three, too—with help from a supportive husband. Sometimes you just have to do these things. But I think, 'If I were on my death bed tomorrow, would I really feel happy about how I spent the last part of my life?' Absolutely! Yes! However, there is still so much to be done.

Claudia: From banking to train driving to book mentoring and publishing. What essential steps got you to this point in your life?

Michelle: First, I needed to get out of my head and stop making things all about me. I was a perfectionist. It stopped me from taking action because I was often worried about not being seen as good enough; everything I did had to be perfect. I had to make what I do about others rather than about myself and my fears. So the first thing I needed to do was recognise what it was that I did well and really enjoyed doing so that, no matter how strenuous it was and how tired I was, I would be happy doing it. And one of the things I'm passionate about is public speaking to make a difference in people's lives. I enjoyed, and still enjoy, speaking from the rostrum and hearing someone call out to me, 'You've inspired me.' Or, 'You've said something that really lights up the bulb inside me.' So I said to myself, 'You know what, I need to do that.' I've also loved writing ever since I was a child, and that's something that other people say I do well.

Then I needed to identify my purpose, the big 'why', or, in other words, what I'm born to do in life. My 'why' has always been about helping people create their desired life. I did not believe that I could have that ability after the challenges that I had gone through. For many of us, that's what holds us back. We think that, with everything that goes on and has gone on in our lives, we don't have the ability to reach a certain level. Obviously, my family are part of my 'why' that keeps me going and believing. Whatever I am doing out there reflects on them and affects them as well. I'm about making a difference to people; for them to believe that, no matter what people say about them, no matter what traumatic experiences they've gone through, no matter what belief they have about themselves, they still have the ability to come back to their own 'why'.

So I attended The Coaching Academy, and I did Master Coaching. I learnt NLP to offer clients extra value. And then I created a circle of influence, excellent people and networks of incredible people who were excelling in their fields or were aiming for brilliance. I could feed off their energy and learn from them. From there, I got involved with a female mastermind group, another great circle of influence, which supported me in building my own business.

I've always been a constant learner. I think the more I learn, the more I'm able to help those that I want to help. Obviously, I had to map out where I really wanted to be and choose to learn what I needed to do to get there. In life, even though we come from certain backgrounds, we're never fully aware of where our potential can take us. That's what I believe. We are all a work in progress. I always say to myself, 'I'm a building under construction.' It's constant growth. I think if you stop growing and learning, you're dead because there has to always be something more for you. You could be in the same job or the same line for a while, and you make a decision to grow, to change, to improve something, whether it is your finances, your health, whatever. It's about taking little steps to make yourself better on your journey to realise your 'why'.

Claudia: You've just shared your essential steps, but there must have been a one really significant thing that got you into your current position. What was it?

Michelle: Writing my first book about domestic abuse, openly and honestly, was very significant. I'd been holding in stuff about the abuse. So I wasn't being real. People just saw me with makeup on, bubbly and always running jokes but didn't know what was going on beneath the surface. When I was writing that book, nobody around me knew. I didn't tell anyone, not even my family. I told them when the book was launched. They didn't know half of what was in there, either. They didn't know half of what I went through until my book was out and I did my first TV interview. The first time I spoke about my challenges was at my book launch. It was a massive thing because I always worried about what other people thought of me and how I looked in their eyes. And that's not good because you're not being you. I've always said that it's much more work being fake than being real. Now I enjoy being myself—being real. If you're going to work with me, work with me because of who I actually am, not because of who I portray myself to be. If you're going to be friends with me, let it be the same thing. Being my real self was a huge step for me.

I'm an action taker. Once I get an idea, or someone gives me an idea, I'm gone with it. I don't hesitate. And that's something that really helped me. After I'd signed up with a book writing network, they helped me create a lot of media releases and letters to a lot of radio and TV stations. I really put myself out there, and I was always ready to speak about the book. I remember being at home once, and somebody called and said, 'Can I speak to you in five minutes?', And I said, 'Yes,' even though I didn't know it was going to be a live radio interview. It was an hour live radio interview, and he asked, 'Are you up for this?' And I was like, 'Yes.' No hesitation. If I had said 'no', I might have missed that opportunity. So I would say to anybody be ready at all times for anything.

When I decided to speak out through my book and on stage, people began saying, 'I'm in that position, can you help me?' And then I got my first paying clients, lots of media attention, and a letter of recommendation from the Queen for my book.

Claudia: With all your achievements, Michelle, you must have faced your fair share of challenges. What was your greatest challenge as a black woman?

Michelle: The domestic abuse was definitely my greatest challenge, and that's something that could happen to any woman, regardless of her colour. I didn't know the abusive side of my husband when I married him. I couldn't see it, as I was so much in love with him. So when the abuse started, I really thought I could change him. But instead, he changed me by controlling and abusing me. My confidence went downhill. I was walking on eggshells, not knowing what would upset him next. I stayed in that relationship for as long as I could, believing that he would change. It was hard to be a good parent to my children, too, because abuse saps your energy and lowers your self-esteem. I remember locking myself in the bathroom one day when I was near the end of my tether and thinking, 'Are you going to allow your children to go through this for the rest of their lives?' That's when I decided to leave for good. But even after I left, the abuse continued. He would stalk and harass me. He would damage my things or lock me in the house.

I felt really guilty because my children were missing their dad and were asking for him. I had to deal with the menace and mayhem he was creating even after I'd left. On top of all that, I lost my job, and I had to deal with the debts I was left with. I had to deal with my son and his challenging behaviour, and I had to deal with my guilt. I became very depressed. Although my children kept me going, I saw myself as a problem to other people. I thought that taking my own life would remove me and make everything fine. But it didn't work, and thank God I'm still here.

What I've learned in the steps that I've taken to grow and change is that sometimes you think that you've let go of a bad situation. You believe that you've moved on. Sometimes you think that you've forgiven someone who has hurt you. But actually, you haven't done any of those things at all. You've just put a plaster over the hurt. Over these past few years, that was something I learned about myself. I had to really go deep within myself and find that self-awareness to say, 'You know what? I've forgiven my ex to a point, and I may not be feeling bitter anymore. But I haven't really utilised the opportunity in that situation.' And what I mean here is that I hadn't looked for the benefits in the situation I'd been through and how the situation had helped me. Because we don't do that, right? We look at all the things it took from us and did to us and how badly it affected us. But I've never ever really sat down and made a list of how that experience helped me. Now I know that it made me stronger, more resilient, and it made me pay attention more to who I am as an individual. And my two oldest children came from that relationship. All those benefits, I had never really sat down and paid close attention to how it helped to define me as an individual.

So now, instead of looking back with resentment, I look back with gratitude for where it has taken me. For instance, I don't believe I would have been on this journey now if I hadn't gone through that marriage. That's not to say that all that abuse was good or right. Of course not! But I feel gratitude in knowing that I was able to use that experience to help myself develop a stronger mentality. I didn't have that at the time. Now, if I look back, I can see how much I've grown since then. There is a chance that I might not have grown anyway. It is possible. It's like you are on a journey and then you see this massive hole, and you think, 'Oh my God, I'm going to have to change direction; it's going to take me another long hour,' so, at that time, you're angry and upset about it. But then you go down another route, and guess what? You come across a pot of gold. Sometimes you still argue about the inconvenience that hole caused instead of looking at the fact that, if you hadn't seen that hole and hadn't taken the long way around, you wouldn't have found that pot of gold. 'Every cloud has a silver lining,' they say. As bad as a situation might be, if you look for the silver lining, you will find it. There always is one.

As a black woman, people constantly expect me to be strong, just like the stereotype. Maybe that expectation is placed on black men, too. A speaker I was listening to recently was talking about the fact that when you go to the hospital, sometimes you are ignored as a black woman because they think that you're strong and should just get on with it. So sometimes, you don't get the right level of service from the NHS. As a black individual, I found it shameful to tell somebody that I was being abused or beaten. I'm not sure what it's like for white women, but I know that, for us, because of the effect of that strong black woman stereotype which many black people have unconsciously bought into, we feel this massive shame. On top of that is the effect of experiencing coercive control and violence, which takes away your sense of self and your self-esteem. And that affected me so much that I remained silent, put up a front and smiled, whilst, internally, I was slowly dying. For many people that take their own life, it's because of what's happening internally. People would be like, 'How could they think of doing that?' I was smiling on the outside, but inside I was in turmoil because I had not spoken out because of shame. That expectation that black women have to be strong is always there within me.

The first place I reached out to was my own black community. Although I thought I would be looked down on because of that expectation to be strong or have my shame intensified, that was where I got help. So my first step was taken in the black community and within my church setting. Both embraced me and supported and encouraged me. And thank God I was lucky enough to get that help as an individual. But, obviously, not many people have that opportunity.

Claudia: Being self-aware and reflective, you've probably gained a lot of insight along the way. What would you say was your greatest lightbulb moment?

Michelle: My greatest lightbulb moment came when I joined Andy Harrington's Professional Speakers' Academy (PSA). I've never been shy and was in the school drama group, so I was used to speaking to an audience. But I never saw myself as a 'wow' speaker. I remember my first time at PSA when one of the coaches said, 'How long have you been in PSA?' I said, 'It's my first time,' and she said, 'What?!' Everybody in the group started clapping, and I was like, 'Whoa, am I actually this good?'

People started asking, 'Do you speak at events?' And I was like, 'No, I don't.' I didn't realise that that reply was closing the door on myself because I didn't recognise my potential. So I started speaking at events and creating my own. I talk about overcoming challenges, being an action taker, and using your book as a brand and business marketing tool. I speak about parenting because I have a child with special needs.

I used to think I should be speaking to one particular group, but not anymore because, in every walk of life, no matter their background, people go through different challenges and situations. And that's the first thing that I normally speak about: overcome and rise above, right? And it's about overcoming and rising above whatever the situation or the problem is. Obviously, lately, because I'm now a book coach, I have found myself speaking mainly to entrepreneurs or small business owners about writing a book. But, with regards to the more traditional side of it, my market could be anybody.

Claudia: Now, let's talk about the crucial asset or resource you needed to enable your success. What was it?

Michelle: First and foremost, the greatest resource to me before anything else is God—my Christianity and relationship with God have kept me through some of the most difficult periods of my life, and I have to mention that before anything else because, without that, nothing else would be possible. One resource that was crucial on my journey was definitely Andy Harrington's Professional Speakers Academy. That's where I learned to create my business, where I got the belief and boldness to be a speaker. Gone are my doubts. In my family and my close network, there is no one on a similar journey. Everyone has chosen to be employees rather than business owners, and that's ok. They are satisfied with what they are doing. But I don't want that for me. I want something more, something different.

So far, I've won numerous awards at the Professional Speakers Academy. Also, I've met members who are on a similar journey, and I've partnered with some who have spoken at my events. Being part of the Academy has given me lots of new ideas and many joint venture opportunities.

The thing about the Professional Speakers Academy is that there is a lot of genuine joy when Andy or any of the coaches see a coachee of theirs doing well. They find out what they can do to complement their coachee's success as opposed to trying to knock it down or get the coachee to do something that will benefit their coaching businesses. That doesn't sit well with me because I'm about helping other people. And something else I noticed in another speakers' group I joined before discovering Andy Harrington's PSA (and it might have been a colour thing); the leader never saw that my products and their volume were worth pushing to the forefront. So it was okay for me to run the webinar training for him, but when it came to doing the licenced speaker part of it, no matter how many applications I put in, I never got a response. Never! It was always other people, white people, who got a response. And I would see people who I knew didn't speak as well as I get the spotlight (and I'm not showing off here). You can spot when someone is better than or not as good as you. And I saw this constantly in that group, and I never got feedback as to why. Also, at that group's events, I never ever saw a single black or Asian person being put forward to speak at events, no matter how much we applied for it. A few of us applied, and a few of us ended up leaving.

I got really deflated by all this stuff. But then it reached the point where I realised I had to be my own voice again in the same way, that I was helping other people to find their voices. I used to tell them, 'Don't let stigma hold you back.' I had to walk the talk and do that for myself. Sometimes we coach people, but we don't use the same tools for ourselves. So I had to start using my own tools on myself. What would I have said to a mentee if they had faced this kind of problem and wanted to know what to do? I would have said to them, 'Go for it. Go out there and create your own platform.' So that's what I had to tell myself literally. And that's what I did.

The other crucial resource on my journey was my church. It has been a strong source of spiritual support, particularly after I attempted to take my life. God has been an anchor for me, and He gave me the strength to cope with the challenges that came with my depression and experiences further down the line. He gave me light when life was dark. My faith helped me believe that I could survive through it. And I got peace of mind which, somehow, increased my ability to cope and deal with difficulties in life.

Claudia: There's no doubt, Michelle, that you are a leader. What do you understand by leadership?

Michelle: Leadership is when you're followed by others, and you're leading by example. A leader is open and honest, and bold enough to admit to making mistakes. When a leader gives the impression that nothing should ever go wrong, followers feel pressured to be perfect. That's not a good leader. A good leader is realistic and doesn't expect perfection because it doesn't exist.

A leader has a vision. Mine is to help people because if I didn't have help and support when I needed it, I wouldn't be where I am today. So I want to be a leader who's reachable, who sets an example, and inspires others to do well. Good leaders are truly authentic, too. They are true to who they are, and people are much more likely to trust them, approach them, and listen to them. In my videos, I always talk about #bereal. The people that I coach, the people that have appreciated me the most, are the people that have said, 'I've never felt judged coming to speak to you. I've never felt like I can't be open with you and tell you why I've not taken the action that I was supposed to.' And that's very important to me.

Claudia: And what difference do you think it's made being a leader who is a black woman?

Michelle: Being a black woman leader has definitely made a difference. And there are pros and cons. For instance, being a leader can affect your marriage and your husband's ego—especially if you're very successful and he isn't. I've seen that happen. Also, some people tend to see women leaders as being arrogant and proud, even when they aren't. Maybe that's a stereotype thing. I've come across women leaders who are humble, and people are drawn to them. I find women are more caring and emotional, and followers are sometimes able to resonate a lot more with them than with men.

There are people who dislike being led by a woman—again, a gender inequality thing. They expect men to be leaders but not women. But why should gender matter? What's important is the impact that person has on your life and the connection between you and their openness and honesty.

What I've noticed about the black leadership community is that there seems to be a lack of upliftment and support for black women. I don't know if this exists within the white community, but we have to speak for where we are. I find it really annoying when I see black leaders who find it so hard to lift up black women, right? If somebody sends them something bad about black women, they share it with other people in a flash. Even if they don't know the person, they should be reaching out to that woman, and they should be saying, 'I've seen this; do you need my support?', instead of allowing them to be shredded to pieces. How can you trust leaders who are prepared to see other people who look like them get hurt and even collude with it? If trust in your leader is not there, it's going to be very hard to follow them.

Some people say that it's due to our conditioning as black people. But it's also a matter of choice, right? I can choose to tear Claudia down, or I can choose to lift her up. When I see her doing something great, I can choose to celebrate, applaud her, and not just comment negatively on her social media post if she said something that I disagree with. And there are some people who don't give a shout out to black women who help them. They see it as, 'If I raise Claudia up, potential customers might go to her business or her presentation rather than come to mine.' When others of the same culture and ethnicity as me try to tear me down, I remain positive by allowing myself to know and accept that this is expected; people will be people at the end of the day, regardless of their race and gender. In life, I have come to realise that you cannot take everything to heart; you cannot manage or dictate the actions of others. You only have control over yourself and your own state. Therefore, you are not in control of other people's actions, but you are in control of your reaction. You can choose to let what they do affect you positively or negatively. There are individuals that are going through life carrying heavyweight baggage and they are looking for outlets—people to unload them on. So you must ask yourself, 'Do I really want to carry their load?' Because when you take on board what they do, then that is exactly what you are doing—carrying other people's deadweight. You can either remain in the passenger seat, allowing them to take control of your wheel, or you can make that decision to sit in the driver's seat.

I've noticed that millennials praise each other a lot more than people from my generation. A friend of mine suggested that this lack of upliftment started in slavery days. In order for me to look good in the eyes of my slave master, I needed to show him that I wasn't like the other slaves; I was better. That makes sense to me.

Then we have black people who are more inclined to spend their money with somebody of another colour whose business is the same as yours. I've had that same experience. Somebody did that and it didn't work out and they had to come back to me. I thought to myself, 'What stopped you from making that decision in the first place?' I couldn't see what the difference was between me and the person she chose to go to. Sometimes it's probably a case of believing that the white person knows more because they are white.

Claudia: You're likely to be a role model to other women, and definitely to your daughters. Which leader is your role model?

Michelle Obama is definitely my role model. Specifically, I love her resilience. I think reading her book made me love her even more. You know what I love? She shows what true leadership is, even when Donald Trump and other people were saying nasty things about her. This is, again, about being real, being authentic, and not replying by putting people down. She is very open about how it made her feel, which many people wouldn't expect. They might think that leaders shouldn't show their feelings.

Also, in her book, *Becoming*, she talks about when she realised that people weren't really connecting with her talk because she was saying what she thought they wanted to hear as opposed to how she really felt. That stuck with me in a massive way. But the way that she stood by her husband and guided her family is amazing. I love that woman!

T.D. Jakes is another role model. He's a pastor and a motivational speaker, and he's real. He doesn't care what anybody thinks about him. His main thing is what God thinks of him. That has always been his main talk. 'I'm not here to be a people pleaser; I'm here to be a people supporter, a guide, a leader.' That's another thing—many of us aim to please everyone, and we know that's not possible.

I put up a post on social media recently that we're not cut out to help everyone. The people that you're cut out to help may not be the same people that I'm cut out to help. That's why I believe there is no need for competition. There are enough people in the world for us all. And the way that T.D. Jakes breaks down the word of God is just phenomenal. He reads a scripture, and the revelation that he gets from it brings it to life very clearly, which is what good leaders and good public speakers ought to do—communicate clearly. And what I also love about him is that he's always available to reach out because he doesn't see himself as being too high and mighty.

And yes, both of my role models are black. But I didn't even think about that consciously until now. But maybe I can relate to them more because they are people who look like me and whose experiences resonate with me.

Claudia: You're definitely a relatable woman, particularly to women of colour. So they're likely to heed your advice. What are your three top tips for black and Asian women who want to be leaders in their field?

Michelle: First, be real and honest and open. Because getting on in the world is often tough for women, many of us sell our morals and personal beliefs that we stand for. Although these things remain within us, some of us silence them so we can fit in or get by because of our ambitions. I've always said that, if I can't be me and get the position I want, then that position wasn't meant for me. And whatever you do, don't change in order to fit in, because at the end of the day, you will always be who you are, and you will only be accepted for who you are. The moment that you can no longer be the person they want you to be—because it's tough being someone else—you'll be dropped. And that's the truth. So, don't do what people want you to do, or give an impression of yourself that people want you to give but aren't you. Just be accepted for who you are as a woman.

Your colour doesn't make you any less of a person. For many women of colour, especially those from an African, Caribbean, or Asian background, we have been taught that we have to work ten times harder to achieve. Although this is correct in some respects, I dislike that it has been drilled into us. The message right there implies that we are different and need to make up for that difference. I believe that the art of perseverance and belief in oneself is a stronger message to teach.

Black women often believe they have to work harder than men and white women to get what they want. They have to fit into a certain clique to get there quicker. This means that when you arrive, you didn't get there as you. And just as you changed to get there, you'll change when you're there. That's probably the reason why some women managers are on a power trip; they have to show they're in charge. I've experienced this many times.

My second tip is to believe in yourself. Develop your confidence and you won't be intimidated by anyone or anything that's going on around you. When you believe in yourself, you can be yourself. You're more likely to succeed.

As women of colour, we need to believe in ourselves more because, out in the world, we don't hear enough positives about ourselves. The racism and abuse we experience contribute towards creating self-limiting beliefs. Many of us are only ever told to go and get our education; get a good job, and that's our limit, right? But, deep inside, we know we have the ability to do so much more and achieve a lot more. But the first thing many of us think is that we can't make it to a higher level in our careers or businesses, or we won't be accepted because we are operating in a white world. Believing in yourself helps you to see that maybe you can't get onto somebody else's platform. But guess what? You can go out and create your own, just like Oprah Winfrey. As a black woman, if she had said, 'This is the farthest I can get to,' she would not be where she is today.

But it's not easy to develop self-belief. There's a quote that says, 'Sometimes you have to believe other people's belief in you in order to start believing in yourself.' When you are in your own bubble, it's often hard to be objective and notice what's happening with you. It's about holding onto the lifelines that people give you when they support and praise you until you can find the ability to do that for yourself.

Finally, commit to what you're doing. It's all about your 'WHY'. For example, why are you a leader? Don't just become a leader because you like the word or because you've been put there. Be a leader because it's a way of achieving your 'WHY'. So commit to your 'why' because you're going to have those challenging moments, especially when you face racism and sexism. You're going to be told that you are inferior because of the colour of your skin. Or people in your family might say, 'Are you joking? Are you really going to go for that position?' Or, 'You won't get anywhere because you're black, right?' So your 'why' has to be strong enough that, when those moments come, you don't just quit.

Look at all our great leaders: the Rosa Parks, the Martin Luther Kings. It was their 'why' that made them stand tall. Did they know there was a possibility of being humiliated, lynched, or killed? Of course, they knew. Of course, they were afraid. But their 'why' was bigger than that fear. It gave them the strength to stand for their beliefs. Being a black or Asian woman leader has lots of challenges. Your 'WHY' will keep you going.

'I gave up driving trains in 2019 because, although it was exhilarating, it was not my purpose. I'm now on a mission to change lives.'

— Michelle

CHAPTER 7

Sherry: The Director of Children's Services

Stereotypes cause anguish in the lives of people of colour! They are gross generalisations that disregard individual differences and contribute towards limiting the life chances of their victims. Stereotypes can be emotionally damaging.

Subservient, reserved, unassertive, meek, passive, followers rather than leaders, and unwilling to assimilate: these are commonly held stereotypes of South Asian women, even today. And yet, if you consider the likes of Malala Yousafzai, Benazir Butto, and even the reviled Priti Patel, you're bound to conclude that these stereotypes definitely don't apply. In fact, they blatantly conflict with reality.

This particular Page 1 Woman has been subjected to more than her fair share of stereotypes. Starting her professional life as a nursery nurse teacher, she was talent-spotted early on. Despite being a single mum of two young children, she seized the opportunity offered without hesitation. She quickly climbed the organisational ladder, clearly very competent, very smart, and definitely a leader. And yet, throughout her professional life, she has been challenged by individuals intent on stereotyping her. The higher she scaled her organisational career ladder, the greater the challenge became.

Meet Sherry Malik. She is a woman who is neither subservient nor unassertive, neither meek nor passive—the exact opposite, in fact. She's a woman with a voice, and she's fearless in using it. She fits none of the stereotypes that the Western world has created about women like her. Yet, whenever she joined a new organisation in a management and leadership role, stubborn stereotypes of what she ought to be like have persisted.

Sherry has an unconventional professional trajectory created by design rather than by accident. She makes five-year career plans. She's a risk-taker who doesn't miss opportunities when she sees them. She is a purposeful leader who believes in democratising leadership by developing her staff to lead themselves. And although being stereotyped has, in the past, threatened to hold her back, she has gone on to break through that organisational double-glazed glass ceiling, an oftentimes insurmountable obstacle for many black and Asian women.

Want to know more about the self-assured Sherry Malik? Keep reading.

Since interviewing Sherry for this book, she has taken retirement. She continues to make an impact as a non-executive director of Dimensions UK[16] and is a Trustee at the Internet Watch Foundation[17].

Sherry is also involved in other meaningful activities as a trustee at Social Work Awards and is an associate of Staff College.

---

16 Dimensions UK, a not-for-profit organisation supporting people with learning disabilities, autism, challenging behaviour and complex needs.

17 Internet Watch Foundation minimises the availability of online child sexual abuse content hosted anywhere in the world, and non-photographic child sexual abuse images hosted in the UK.

THE INTERVIEW

Claudia: Sherry, what's your profession?

Sherry: I started as a nursery nurse teacher, and I'm now a Director of Children's Services. I'm responsible for the development and service delivery and scale-up of programmes across the UK for the NSPCC—the National Society for the Prevention of Cruelty to Children. The programmes we are developing are to prevent children from being abused and to recover from abuse and trauma. They are all evidenced and researched, and when they are proven to be effective, we scale them up across the country. We now work across more than 250 sites around the country, scaling up seven of our programmes.

I see my role as supporting and enabling my own teams to do the best they can every day. That's my job as a leader really. When I started in this role five years ago, I inherited a team of 13 senior managers running different regions around the UK. And what I found was that each manager was very good at what they were doing in their own little silos, with their own teams, but they were not thinking about or taking responsibility for the service as a whole. They were not looking at the entire programme and how it could impact children's social care in the UK.

I suppose they all had their own politics with each other as well, which is normal in these big organisations.

Claudia: That must have been demanding at the start. How did you deal with it?

Sherry: Individual team members would often come to me if they were annoyed or upset at a colleague's behaviour and expect me to take some action. Having just finished a coaching course, I took a coaching attitude to it. This meant asking questions to help them to explore the issue and take responsibility to resolve it themselves. For example, 'So, what conversation have you had with him/her?' Or, 'What would you like me to do about it?' If your experience has been that it is your manager's job to resolve conflict, then you won't have the permission or skills to relate to colleagues as adults and to have grown-up conversations with them. I was able to help them practice that conversation with each other so that it landed in the right way by asking, 'Okay, what would you say to her?' I would encourage them to share with that individual the impact their actions had had on them in a non-judgemental way. 'When you did/ said this, it made me feel...' This approach was incredibly productive and helped people to come together as a team.

Fast forward to five years, and what I have is an incredibly strong team, all of whom take responsibility for what we are doing as a whole. We have projects that are cost-cutting, and the managers see and care about the benefit to the whole directorate. They look at quality assurance and data across the directorate. They look at complaints, inspections, and the learning from these across the whole rather than in their own silos. They look at how to manage our communication across the organisation and with stakeholders because our work is quite complicated and isn't always very well understood. We have projects about increasing productivity across the whole directorate. Generally, one person takes the lead, and they work with their colleagues to do a task and finish group reporting to the team as a whole. And they have worked incredibly well in establishing the strategy for the next 10 years.

I would say that it is a very high-functioning team. We lean on each other for support. I know that I had a role in bringing this about, which people recognise when they say, 'It wasn't always like that, Sherry. You've enabled us.'

My job was to give them the information to make the best decisions for themselves. They are a really good-humoured bunch. We have great fun when we get together, and managed to maintain that even during the period of COVID-19 and lockdown with workshops on Zoom.

Claudia: So, how did you get into social work?

Sherry: Well, it's a long story. I grew up in India and later moved to California. I had two children during the six years I was living there. I went to evening classes and qualified as a pre-school teacher, working part-time during the day. And when I returned to the UK, I started to work for Barnet, a London local authority. I was a single mum at the time. I was managing a small day nursery for the local authority, so it kind of fit with what I was previously doing in America. Then my talent was dutifully spotted, and I was offered an opportunity when the assistant director asked if I would like to be seconded to do a social work course. I could have easily said, 'No', because I was a busy single mother with two children under the age of six. And I wasn't in a good place at that point in my life. But I thought about it for about a nanosecond and said, 'Yes.' I said to myself, 'I'll find a way to manage all this and my children.' This is the thing about life: if you don't grab the opportunities when they come, you'll miss them and end up full of regrets.

I knew that if I wanted to do the social work course, I would have to work incredibly hard. I had to fight to get a place at the London School of Economics (LSE) because my employer didn't want to pay the fees. They suggested I go to a polytechnic instead, where the fees were lower. But I knew the LSE was prestigious and a good course, so I said, 'I'll find the money myself for the difference in the fees.' It wasn't a lot of money overall, but it was a big deal for me in those days because I was struggling financially. I suppose I saw it as making an investment in myself and having a good qualification from a really reputable university was very important to me. When I left India aged 19, my father made sure I had a bachelor's degree and driver's licence. Both, he thought, would give me independence and a career. So having the chance to do an MSc was a gift and an opportunity to make my dad proud. And I never looked back.

Claudia: Your dad must have been really proud. What other essential steps got you to where you are now?

Sherry: I qualified as a social worker in 1991. Fast forward to 2020, and I have somehow amassed nearly 30 years of experience in so many different settings. The last 16 of these have been at the director level. So what can I tell you about how I got here?

First, I followed my passion—when I picked my next move, I didn't just ask if I could do the job. Rather, I asked myself if I would learn, develop, and grow here. My CV doesn't look like an obvious career trajectory—I've moved between local government, third sector, audit and inspection, central government bodies, and regulation. For example, I moved from local government to working for a charity, and although I was getting a slight promotion, I had to take a cut in salary at that time. But I didn't mind because it was going to be a completely different experience and new context. Every move was a bit out of my comfort zone in the beginning, but that stretch always helped me to grow and learn and take a broader approach to my work.

Second, I also always had a bit of a plan. There was always some personal goal I was aspiring to. It didn't mean that I stuck to it 100 per cent, but it was always there in the background as my compass—'This is where I want to be in five years. And one day, I want to be leading an organisation.' It was incredibly helpful because it was like a little driver to help me make the right decisions along the way. So when I got the opportunity to be seconded to do the social work training course, I immediately said 'Yes.' When I got the opportunity to get a management qualification, I said 'Yes.' People were saying, 'Oh, you're going to leave local government. What about your pension?' I was like, 'Okay. Well, I'm quite young. I don't have to worry about my pension right now. I want to go and learn something completely different and new.' I took advantage of those opportunities because they were part of my plan to do interesting things, learn, and bring something more constructive to the job.

Twice I moved within the year from positions where I didn't feel comfortable or which were not right for me. Some people say they wouldn't do that because it would look bad on their CV, so they stay put even though things aren't right. I think that is a mistake. I never regretted leaving those places because they were causing me stress and diminishing my confidence. I always made sure I had a coach to help me make the right decisions and make sense of what was happening.

Third, if you really want to do something, your life will expand to make space for it. I wanted to serve as a non-executive director on a board and negotiated the time with my CEOs. This helped me gain experience in health, private, and public sector settings. I did this alongside the day job, arguing that I would bring back learning from other sectors and that this was part of my development. It always paid off. Working across so many different sectors helped me to develop a broad network. I have worked at maintaining this and using it to connect people and share learning.

Fourth, 'how to be' is just as important as 'what to do'. I have learnt that being kind, being empathetic, showing humanity, and showing vulnerability—are qualities that make you a better leader. Some colleagues I have worked with see that as a sign of weakness and will position themselves to appear as stronger and more capable. Life happens to all of us—death, divorce, illness. But somehow, we are meant to deny this aspect of our lives at work and not let it affect our performance. We don't want to share those personal aspects of our life, which may reveal our vulnerabilities, because we want to be seen as professional and competent, especially if the leadership culture in the workplace is a macho one.

More than 20 years ago, my parents died in a car accident in India. I had just changed jobs and was six months in. I was feeling confident and beginning to make my mark, and then my world collapsed.

I can only describe what happened next as a surge of empathy from colleagues, friends, and my employer, a large national charity. The kindness came in many forms—letters, cards, flowers, hugs, permission to cry, permission to take time out. When I returned to work, I found I couldn't concentrate, couldn't remember being in meetings or discussing issues. A fog had descended on my brain, and I couldn't see, hear, or feel anything clearly other than thinking about what had happened. Eventually, I asked my employer if I could take three months unpaid leave so I could return to India and sort out my parents' affairs.

My colleagues, my manager, and the organisation itself were hugely supportive of my decision to take time out. Without my having to ask, the head of HR worked out a combination of annual, unpaid, and compassionate leave for three months and ensured that the loss of salary was spread out over 12 months, so I did not feel the impact.

Three months later, I returned quite refreshed. The fog I had been under earlier had lifted because I had been given time to deal with my trauma without guilt or worry about work. I continued to experience thoughtfulness and had permission to talk about my grief with colleagues who stopped to ask—really ask—how I was. Their kindness gave me the strength to come to work, be engaged, and do my best every day.

So, in my experience, kindness and being yourself creates trust. I have never forgotten how it feels to receive kindness and have always offered the same kindness to colleagues I have worked with because good relationships mean we can do much better for those we support.

The final point I want to make is, every crisis is an opportunity. I joined the General Social Care Council (GSCC), the previous regulator for social workers, in 2010 as the deputy CEO. Within two months, the newly-elected coalition government announced that they were closing us down. At that point, I had a choice to leave or to lead. I learnt that if you focus on the purpose, the rest follows. Staying at the GSCC and closing the organisation really helped me learn a lot about how to lead in the face of crisis.

The COVID-19 pandemic has been a crisis for the whole world. We are seeing world leaders who are rising to the occasion and others... well, not so much! Every crisis teaches us we can be innovative, creative, and resilient as leaders.

Claudia: Social work is a challenging profession for anyone who chooses it as a career. What challenges did you experience along the way as a woman of colour? And how did you overcome them?

One of the things I learnt along the way is that I will always have to work twice as hard to be judged just as good as my white colleagues. I know many other black and Asian colleagues who feel similarly.

What I often noticed is that if a white person gets the job, it's assumed that they can do it, and they come into the job with the confidence and approval of their colleagues. There's no questioning of their ability to do the job. But my experience has been that, in some quite subtle ways, and perhaps it's because I don't fit the stereotype of an Asian woman, I always had to prove that I could do the job before I was recognised for my ability, and people then expressed their confidence in me.

One of the stereotypes of South Asian women is that we are compliant, soft-spoken, and unassertive. And I guess, because I'm of a small build, I lead with authority, I am confident about my knowledge and skills, even though it makes some people uncomfortable. I know my job and I'm not shy about doing it. These qualities would be admired in a white person. But, as an Asian woman, I had to work hard to establish trust, and then I have to do it all again each time someone new comes into the team.

When I was younger, it used to make me really angry and annoyed. I would get a bit defensive about it, and I probably sometimes still do. But I've learned, as people of colour, we have to intentionally choose how to respond to situations where we are the only other person of colour in our teams, or at the senior table, and someone says or does something that makes you feel lesser. I guess that you've got to understand people's motivations for the questions that they are asking. It's best to address this by taking a coaching stance, to ask open questions, to clarify rather than take it personally. You've got to believe in yourself and remind yourself of the successes you've had, the things that you have achieved; otherwise, your confidence gets a knock.

When I arrived at Cafcass (the Children and Family Courts Advisory and Support Service), it was in utter chaos and turmoil, having been set up as a brand new organisation not long before. I quickly convinced the CEO that I was not only the right person for that job but also to change my role very quickly so that I could make the most of what I brought to the table from the Audit Commission. I worked incredibly hard to put basic systems in place that hadn't existed previously. I had been a senior inspector and auditor at the Audit Commission, and I applied this experience of what a good organisation should look like to my job at Cafcass. I worked there for six years, and I was the only woman of colour in the corporate directors' team.

One of the stereotypes that black and minority ethnic professionals face is that they are seen as the people with all the answers around diversity and inclusion. We are not experts on this topic and have only our own experiences to inform us. Many of us want to be seen as experts in our profession and not be tasked with becoming diversity experts because we happen to be black or Asian, and no one else seems to know how to do it.

At Cafcass, however, I had the director's responsibility to ensure that equality, diversity, and inclusion were central to our work. So I set up a national steering group. The one thing I didn't want the group to be was a talking shop, and I didn't want it to be solely about learning. I wanted it to be about action, making change, and improving practice. I wanted it to be firmly rooted in social work and to be beneficial to the work Cafcass was doing. We instigated research projects to help us understand what our black, Asian, and minority ethnic service users were experiencing. Then we put that research out to the regions and helped people to improve their practice on that basis. The whole idea was to give confidence to our staff to work with confidence with black and minority ethnic children, and to understand and respect the principles of equality and diversity more broadly.

Claudia: You must have had lightbulb moments along the way, Sherry. Tell us, what was your most significant lightbulb moment?

Sherry: Actually, Cafcass was a lightbulb moment because, when I got there and moved into a national role, I blew up that glass ceiling. You know, I was suddenly in the corporate team, earning a really good salary, which I needed at that time to get my life back on track, as I was going through a divorce. I nearly lost my home during that period, but having a good salary meant that I could get a mortgage and pay off those marital debts.

I really felt like I had broken the glass ceiling at that point; I was a person of colour, and I was a woman as well, and I was in a senior position. I had earned it. I was actually enjoying the huge challenge of the job and feeling that I was getting more confident in what I was doing every day because that's the other thing that many of us women feel—that imposter syndrome. How did I get here? And, 'Oh my God, can I actually do this? Will I get found out?' I had plenty of that, but one of the things I learned in the Audit Commission was that we will always work out how to solve a problem.

I had a structure and a framework in my head that I learned from the Audit Commission. So, at Cafcass, I took on things like risk management, business planning, managing national information systems and performance management, quality assurance, things that I hadn't done on that large scale before. But my experience at the Audit Commission was incredibly useful in helping me to think, 'What I really need because I can't do it myself; I've got to set up ways to involve other people to make this thing happen.' That framework worked incredibly well.

When I was a younger manager, I mostly managed upwards and made sure I had the approval of my seniors and that they knew the achievements of my team. When I got a senior position in Cafcass, I realised that if I really wanted to get something done, I had to largely focus on convincing a massive group of staff dispersed across the country that it was the right thing to do. I recognised that I was nothing without the approval of my staff.

That lightbulb moment came when I was doing the quality assurance work, putting a suitable framework in place and convincing people. One day, as I was on one of my many trips to a Cafcass team in the country doing a roadshow on the quality assurance framework somewhere in the West Country, a social worker challenged me, saying he was long in the tooth and didn't need a young inexperienced manager to come along and tell him how to do social work. (The cheek of him!) So I said to him, 'How do you know you're doing good work?' And he said, 'Because I feel good, and that's all I need.' And I said, 'Well, what you think is good social work may not be what a child or a carer or your manager thinks is good. These systems will help all of us to know what good looks like for everyone.' It landed with everyone else in the team, even though I don't think I convinced him!

That trip made me realise that I really needed to win hearts and minds if I wanted to change things. My job title didn't automatically mean that people were going to follow me. I would have to go out and convince people that I was a leader worth following.

Claudia: Developing as a social worker and then a leader needs resources. What resources were crucial to you on your journey?

Sherry: First, ensuring I was well-informed. This meant that I had to make sure I had the necessary knowledge, that I was up to date on issues in my industry, and that I was talking to those people doing the work on the frontline and learning what was going on there. As

I said, having a job title doesn't give you a guarantee that people will respect you. You really need to be well-informed. But, equally, you're not expected to know everything, especially if you have a broad portfolio in your senior job. You need to own up to yourself that you don't know everything and ask questions. Don't pretend that you know everything because people will see through you, and you will lose respect. Be intelligent about the questions you are asking, and they will come if you genuinely listen and are interested. Colleagues have often told me that they really value being asked questions about the detail of their work.

Secondly, it is essential to develop personal resilience, and what helps is a good support network of colleagues, your family, your friends. You have to find ways to look after yourself. Life and adversity happen to all of us, personally and professionally. So finding ways to de-stress and knowing what that is for you is essential. Maya, my grandchild, is my great leveller. If I have an afternoon or a day with her, it kind of switches me off from work; it's just incredible. I am completely de-stressed once I've had a day with her. I also do a lot of gardening, nature walks, holidays, meeting friends, cooking for people.

I've made a point of working hard at consciously building my network. Every job I've left, I've made friends that I've kept in touch with over time. I might meet people for a coffee or a drink. I'll pass work onto people who are freelancing. Those things are really important because when you need people's support, they'll be there for you equally.

Claudia: Sherry, you've many years' experience as a leader. Tell me, what's your understanding of leadership?

Sherry: Leadership is when you get comfortable in your own skin in your role as a leader. You're not anxious all the time or trying to work by the book or rules. You trust that your experience and instincts will help you make the right decisions; you are kind, you are yourself. When you relax and be yourself, get comfortable in your own skin, people will respond really well to you.

I saw it first in Anthony Douglas, the CEO at Cafcass. He's incredibly comfortable in his own skin. He had a lot of confidence, and he didn't mind cracking jokes to make everyone relaxed. He knew everybody who worked for him; he was very personable, and he helped us relax as managers. He was very much himself in the role.

Things do go wrong at work, of course. It's not like they will never go wrong. But it's how you put them right that defines you. So you need to make sure that you accept responsibility and learn how to say 'Sorry' if need be. You need to be willing to learn from it and say, 'Okay, how can I do it better?' You don't get defensive and shut down and blame other people. Anthony Douglas used to say this to me: 'You will always have to be much more generous to your staff than they will ever be back to you.' That has always stayed in my head when having to make difficult decisions that aren't popular.

To me, social justice and focusing on the mission has always been important. I don't think there are many issues you face in life where there is only one right answer or one way of achieving a positive outcome. Compromise, or trying new ways, is healthy. However, every once in a while, something comes along which just isn't right. And you have to stand up for what you believe in. So, on a few occasions, I have had to summon my courage and do the right thing when it really mattered, even if it meant that my job was on the line. I have never regretted it because I know I would sleep better at night.

People don't become leaders just by virtue of their titles. You have to think, 'Well, if I want to achieve anything, I've got to take all these people with me. I've got to convince them that this is the right direction, the right decision.' To do it well, you need to be authentic; you need to be honest; you need to take responsibility; you need to be ready to say you're sorry; you need to be generous—all those things. But you also need to bring people together, work as a team, and take responsibility for the whole, because one person's success is everybody's success. And when one person fails, they will all pitch in and help put it right without blame.

Claudia: So, as a very experienced leader, what are your top three tips for women of colour who want to be leaders in their field?

Sherry: First, believe in yourself. Sometimes, you're going to feel like a fraud and think, 'I'm going to be found out.' Actually, I've found that a lot of people feel like this, but for women of colour, it can be compounded by experiences of racism or micro-aggressions at work. One technique I developed is to remind myself of all my successes. When I recognise a colleague suffering from this 'imposter syndrome', I tell them to go and read their CV and update it. It helps boost their confidence when they realise they have achieved so much. If you have successes that you can draw on, you can build on that.

Second, related to this imposter syndrome is the syndrome of aiming for perfection. You know, sometimes good enough is good enough. And I know that a lot of people beat themselves up about perfection. One of the managers at the Audit Commission would say to me, 'I don't want perfect; I want it to turn around in time. So, stop trying to perfect this because it's really good, and it's good enough.' I learned from her how to avoid being anxious trying to achieve perfection unnecessarily.

My final tip is to understand people's motivations and address that rather than taking things personally. This is so that you don't misunderstand and you don't have crossed messages. Often, people's questioning of your work can seem like criticism, and that may not have been their intention. So, listen and reflect on what's being said to you. Unpack that with them and just say, 'Help me understand why you want that.' Or 'Can you help me understand what you're worried about?' And that can then help you to have a better dialogue rather than get defensive.

One last word—practice gratitude every day. It reminds us of everything we have and shifts the focus from what we lack. It puts life in perspective.

'There was always some personal goal I was aspiring to. It didn't mean that I stuck to it 100 per cent, but it was always there in the background as my compass—'This is where I want to be in five years. And one day, I want to be leading an organisation."

— Sherry

CHAPTER 8

Netty: The Faith and Money Breakthrough Business Coach

When you're a teenager from an unstable, oppressive background, where mental health issues play a central role, how do you survive out in the wider world? What if this background causes you to rebel and drift into abusive relationships? What if, years later, you find yourself with two children, imprisoned in a cycle of violence, emotional abuse, and coercive control, desperate to escape, but hounded and captured each time you do? What would you do?

'When people say they don't understand how individuals get caught in domestic abuse, [tell them to] come and speak to me.'

Meet Anneth Bryan (also known as Netty), a feisty, determined, and resilient domestic abuse survivor and a gutsy Page 1 Woman. When Netty finally cultivated her personal power and started standing up for herself, the abuse ended abruptly—in a way she couldn't have foreseen. Life has a way of turning the greatest mishaps into the most unexpected opportunities if you care to seek them out.

What we know about domestic abuse is that leaving the abusive environment is far from simple. The abuser chips away at your self-esteem and sense of self, leaving you confused, on a perpetual emotional roller coaster, feeling disempowered and worthless. Often it takes years of torturous steps forward, and then backward, and a massive amount of courage and support to make that final decision to leave.

Netty's is a narrative of tragedy followed by triumph. When she combined her childhood experiences of parental mental health, enduring abuse, and her staunch faith, she turned herself into a savvy, compassionate, and innovative woman with a portfolio business. She found her calling.

'*Now I'm serving others. And the more I've served, the more I've healed. And I've also counselled my children and helped them through their trauma to cope and recover from the aftermath of their father's actions.*'

Here's Netty, an incredibly brave woman.

THE INTERVIEW

Claudia: Netty, describe what you do.

Netty: My business now is faith and money breakthrough business coaching. I specialise in coaching and mentoring ambitious, high-achieving women. I assist them with turning their gifts into fruitful services by creating a highly profitable Expert Signature System®.

They are usually coaches, healers, trainers, or public speakers, but I can work with any service-based entrepreneur who finds it hard to charge what they're worth, who struggles with their money mindset, who has difficulty knowing how to package their offer, and who wrestles with converting prospects into clients, or with bringing their brand voice into their business. I help them to identify their archetypes. They also learn what it takes to monetise their magic and then launch their business. If they are in business already, we look at what the gaps are so we can get them leveraged to the next level quickly, so they start to see the results and transformation needed to lead them towards success. And all by introducing them to the concept of building a profitable Expert Signature System®. This, of course, includes a lot of faith-building and mindset work so that they can connect the business and service delivery from a heart-centred space.

I also specialise in working with women to elevate their mindset and relationship with money by using personal money profiling. Doing this helps them to press *reset* on their old money stories so they can fix it and start looking through the lens of seeing themselves where they want to be rather than where they are presently. I have recently launched a movement called '*Miracle Money Breakthrough Revolution*'. It involves showing the clients in my Money School how to understand their relationship with money, and how this is a catalyst for how they do the rest of their life, because I believe 'how you do money is how you do everything'.

I love serving, empowering, and giving great value to women. I love helping them to raise their faith in themselves and their abilities. I love helping them to see how having what I call 'crazy faith' is a must for pulling them forward in life and in business. I love helping them take their calling out of the box and really work it in the marketplace as God intended.

Claudia: How did you get into a faith-based business?

Netty: I did a variety of things before establishing my current business offering, of course. I was a community mediator for 14 years, a social worker for 18 years, a counsellor, and a pastor of a small vibrant church. But my main thing career-wise was when I found restorative justice work, which I've been doing now for about 10 years. It involves helping those harmed by crime or conflict by giving them the opportunity to meet their harmers and open a dialogue about what happened. It's a great process that helps them cope, recover, and move on. The restorative justice process allows them to ask the 'whys' and 'whats' of their harmers' actions and address the behaviour. I now offer this to women who need it under the 'life' part of my new business model, and this can be in relation to any situation, personal or business.

I also trained foster carers and social care professionals in independent fostering agencies and local authorities on safeguarding and parenting children who'd suffered abuse and trauma. I ran parenting courses and coached young people with severe psychological, emotional, and behavioural difficulties.

My business has evolved in this way because, while I found being a trainer/consultant for foster carers, parents, and young people a joy, it wasn't a viable business model for the big vision I had as an entrepreneur, public speaking mentor, and public speaker. I had to pivot, and I'm glad I did because now I can go back and serve in the areas that I love from a place of abundance and not lack. Based on the last two years of what I've observed in the market, I felt I needed to lead with something different. My lead offering working in business and money coaching drives me because I believe it's very important for people to work for themselves. It's crucial that women especially have the capacity and know-how to create their own economy so that they can do more, get back to their families, and serve in the community they have been called to. That way, they are able to leave legacies for their children as well.

Claudia: How much was your involvement in social care and restorative justice related to your early experiences?

Netty: When I was growing up, my mother had mental health issues and was frequently admitted into psychiatric hospitals. My father often worked away to keep the money coming in. So my two sisters and I regularly stayed with family or church members. It was pretty unstable and very difficult. We'd have the welfare people come around because, due to my mother's illness, she sometimes kept us away from school.

My father was an overly strict Christian who often beat us with his belt and instilled fear within us—abuse by today's standards. But in those days, it was pretty much the norm in many Caribbean, staunchly religious families. I believe it was based on the Bible verse, 'Spare the rod and spoil the child.' But it didn't work for me. It backfired, in fact. So we missed out on the playful side of childhood, our mother's love, and bonding with her. Often, we were forbidden from doing normal, ordinary childhood things, such as going to our friends' homes. We would see our friends going to school discos, and we weren't allowed to go. We would ask if we could go, too, but were always told that we needed to stay home and go to our rooms or read our schoolbooks. I look back on my childhood and think how hard it was, and that I needed more consistency. But my parents did what they did to the best of their ability at that time. And also, things were often swept under the carpet. According to Jamaican culture at the time, we were not allowed to 'chat about our business' outside the family home. That was taboo. So, outside the family, no one really knew what was going on.

At around the age of 13, I rebelled. I didn't have any freedom. I felt stifled, so I literally just broke away, thinking there was more out in the big wide world than there actually was. I started staying out the odd night, which turned into a few nights, then a week, and then a month. Eventually, I went missing for about two years. During that time, I met and lived with older 'friends' who were actually adults and not my friends at all. I didn't know it then, but they groomed me into a life of petty crime by getting me to shoplift for them and making me feel that I belonged there and that I was loved—all the things I wanted from my family at home but didn't get. I got caught by the police on a few occasions for shoplifting, alcohol mostly. It wasn't until I was sitting in a police station, and my father had to come and get me, that I looked at him, and thought, 'Oh my God, what am I doing?' The fear I felt when I saw him really shook me up, and I went back home. And the reprimand that I got on returning home was so severe that it just knocked me for six again. Being glad to be back home didn't last long because things felt worse than when I first left. So it wasn't long before I rebelled and ran away again.

When I met my children's father, Charlie, who was quite a bit older than me, I was 15 ½ and living away from home with friends. He spotted me in a nightclub and went after me. It turned out that he had undiagnosed mental health problems, and the relationship became abusive. I now know that I stayed because of my upbringing—the message was 'Parents stay together, no matter what.' I was controlled by the fear that came from my father, as he made us feel we couldn't do anything right. Fear was my norm.

Several months after meeting Charlie, I got pregnant. Being underage and vulnerable, I went into local authority care but wasn't happy. So I ran away and did a bit of sofa-surfing with friends until I moved to a bedsit with Charlie, just 25 miles down the road from my parents. Being pregnant, I wanted my family and needed my mum, so I returned home. Surprisingly, my parents accepted me, and a couple of months afterwards, I gave birth to my son.

After about a year, I got a flat with Charlie 20 miles away from my parents. Things quickly deteriorated as he became increasingly abusive. As I'd left school without qualifications, I tried to educate myself at night school over the years. However, he tried to sabotage any attempt to better myself. I struggled for years trying to be me in that relationship. But it was always about him and what he wanted. I tolerated his abuse, drug-taking, gambling lifestyle, and the open house he kept where his friends could turn up at any hour of the day or night.

I tried to lead a normal life raising my two children amongst the chaos. When abusing me, he'd lock me in the bedroom, hold me at knifepoint, or beat and degrade me verbally and emotionally in front of his friends. When he knew he'd done something really bad, he'd try to make up by playing happy families. So I was totally confused.

Whenever I left, he'd hunt me down. He even kidnapped our two-year-old daughter and blackmailed me into coming home. Although there were no prison doors or guards, I definitely felt imprisoned. I became so fearful of him in the same way that I was fearful of my father. He had so much power over me that I felt powerless and completely worthless. That's why I stayed for 18 years.

Much later in the relationship, I met an American woman online who I shared my experiences with. She empowered me to start believing in myself, and I worked hard to plan a way out. I had become so much stronger just from sharing my experience with a stranger. I know this might sound crazy, but before then, I didn't really have anybody to talk to who could help me get confident enough to leave.

Then I started to realise the impact of the abuse on my children. I woke up one day and had what you could call an 'insight moment'. I realised that this clock of mine was ticking away, and Charlie had stolen my youth, my adulthood, my womanhood. I realised that my self-esteem was at rock bottom. I had a lot going for me but no confidence. Because of what he'd done to me, I felt completely use-less. And then I began thinking, 'enough is enough'. That's when I started standing up for myself. Whenever he would knock me down, I would get right back up again, and each time stronger. Eventually, his power and control over me started slipping away.

One morning in May 2001, Charlie started to argue with me as I prepared for work. He sabotaged my morning as he usually did in order to get my day off to a bad start. I left home feeling very uneasy. He kept calling me at work throughout the day, and I said, 'I haven't time for this; I'm working. Let's talk later.' Later never came for us. Sometime that day, he took his own life. He did it in a way that was shocking and aggressive, and clearly meant for me to find him. The hardest thing was that it was my 12-year-old daughter who actually found him. She had to get help; she called me and contacted the emergency services.

I got involved in restorative justice, and trauma recovery work for two reasons. First, I wanted victims to be empowered to leave abusive situations. Second, I wanted them to be able to get answers to those questions that my children and I never got to ask Charlie—

for example, why did he do what he did to me? Why did he take his own life? I got involved in social care, and trained as a counsellor because my mum and Charlie both had mental health problems. I was now able to understand my past and how I could use those experiences to help others.

I also went to Bible school and trained as a pastor. And I ran a ministry myself for five years that focused on women and a small local congregation. I even worked as a street pastor for seven years. I did that until my children made me a grandma seven years ago. So the helping profession has always been close to my heart. Helping the disadvantaged, helping the vulnerable, those without a voice, those on the edge, if you like, of society.

Eventually, alongside working as an independent social worker, I set up my own training organisation, Well Springs, that focused on foster care. And then, I decided to focus solely on restorative justice because I found that there was a massive need for it locally, and there wasn't a service provider. So we became the leading non-statuary organisation for restorative practice in our local area, where I trained over 1,000 police officers to implement this strategy in their organisation.

Doing all of these things helped me to get closure on those painful experiences. It's a case of the more I serve others, the more I heal because it's a 'give and you shall receive' kind of thing. And I counselled my own children through their loss and grief and helped them to cope and recover in the aftermath of what their father had done. So it was good to see them grow and develop in their own right because we didn't get any help from any services.

Claudia: Having experienced a tough early life and trauma, your achievements are quite remarkable. What vital steps got you to where you are today?

Netty: Having left school early, with no qualifications, I later did math and English at night school. A few years later, I became an unqualified social worker in a hospital for about five years. I then studied hard for three years. I solidly put my head down and focused because I had to catch up on all that lost time. And, in 2005, I qualified as a social worker and simultaneously got two diplomas—in counselling psychology and theology and leadership. Then, in 2010, I was ordained as a pastor and ran a local church and women's group for several years. When I became a grandma, I took a sabbatical to give time back to my family. I also studied all aspects of restorative practice in dealing with serious and complex cases and harmful sexual behaviours.

In 2017, I joined an academy for professional speakers, and this was really where my entrepreneurial spark took off. I loved being around like-minded business people who were ambitious, high-achievers. I learned everything I was being taught by Andy Harrington, the founder of the academy, and applied it to my business. Then an opportunity came up for me to become one of his mentors. I passed the training and began mentoring others to create wealth from speaking to selling on stage. This role took me abroad to places such as Dubai and Australia, places I had dreamt of travelling to. So I'm helping people on an international scale to develop and grow their public speaking and presentation skills and build a profitable business at the same time.

And then, in 2019, I realised that I needed to change things in my own business. I met a female business coach with who I connected synergistically and spiritually. She really opened my eyes to what I needed to do to elevate myself to the next stage in my life and my career.

So, at the beginning of that year, I invested heavily in some additional coaching and mentoring in order to take my career in a different direction; that is what I'm doing now as a faith and money breakthrough business coach. It turned out to be the best decision I have ever made because it was the icing on the cake of all of the things that I had been doing in the past 30 years. It was just what I needed. It's as if it was the actualization point of my life, career, and business all wrapped into one.

Claudia: With everything you have faced, being a black woman would have brought challenges. What were they, specifically on your career journey? How did you overcome them?

Netty: Once, I was brought before the social work regulatory body due to a manager's false accusation. The whole process, which took a harrowing two years, could have destroyed my career. It placed me back in the same scenario of power and control where I was with Charlie. But I got advice from a lawyer who said, 'You've everything within you to challenge this.' So I represented myself for the five days of the hearing.

With no experience in law, I mirrored the barrister representing the regulatory body. I'd been conscientious with my case recordings and I knew everything. It was the worst and the best experience of my life. Before the hearing, I'd received an anonymous letter saying that the manager was a fraudster and an unethical businessman. It said, if I kept going, I would triumph. It gave me the impetus to carry on.

The panel found no case to answer and congratulated me for the way I'd represented myself. I could continue practicing as a social worker. I won! That experience pushed me to channel the negative energy from two years of depression generated by this matter into re-strategizing my business. And I realised that I didn't need to rely on anybody to create my future. I had the power within me. I thought, 'From this moment on, no one will ever put me down, hire or fire me unless their name is God. I'm a woman of faith, and I'm a woman in control.' When I reflected on the whole experience, I concluded that the manager in question either didn't like me or didn't like my colour. I got offered the role, which I later learned he had been reserving for someone else who was not a woman of colour.

The accusations were religiously charged as well, and the way he spoke to me or about me was no less than degrading. The hardest thing was having to face and cross-examine this man who I hadn't seen for two years, as I had left the role, and the proceedings were lengthy. He did everything to try to make me look small in front of the panel. It was very intimidating. Whether this was racially charged or not, I cannot say for sure, but I felt it. I had a feeling inside that made me feel really uncomfortable.

My most recent big challenge in this area came when I became more involved in public speaking, which is a male-dominated field. It was always being said on social media and in my public speaking network that the public speaking circuit needed more women. But when, as an experienced and qualified black woman speaker, I put myself forward for opportunities, I never ever got picked.

In other places, such as in my work with restorative justice, being a black woman working in public sector organisations has brought a huge number of challenges. Sometimes we go for opportunities offered over and over again. We don't get them, and we have to over-prove ourselves. For example, when I was working within the social care field, I would put myself forward for secondment opportunities and wouldn't get picked even though I was super experienced. I experienced managers talking down to me as if I had no intelligence. This made me feel really uncomfortable, and second-guess myself all the time.

And I find that over-proving is undermining, especially when you don't get picked or you are not valued for the good work you do. This is a challenge that I, as a black woman, struggle with every day—constantly having to prove that I'm good at what I do.

In the past, when I was more vulnerable, and I didn't have as much resilience, these challenges would cut deep. Now that my resilience is greater, I try not to see these things as obstacles. Maturity has helped me to stop worrying about what people think. So I manage and deal with these kinds of challenges so much better.

Having to historically over-prove myself, I believe, has delayed my progress as a public speaker and a business owner. I know I'm good at what I do because I get great feedback every time. I have even been told I am world-class by a very prominent person in the professional speaker's field, but I know I don't step out as much as I could. So, the knock-on effect is that I've not progressed as quickly as I could have done. For example, I recently started a new venture in business, which I could have started maybe 12 months earlier. Maybe I've held myself back because of my own self-limiting beliefs about my value and my worth. Sometimes that little voice in my head questions whether I am as good as the next person. Maybe it's to do with my past experiences of having been abused by two important men in my life. Or perhaps it's a combination of the two. I was a black girl who was made to feel worthless, who was held back and not allowed to be herself. So that would have affected my beliefs about my value in this world. And when racism and sexism kick in in my work, I'm taken back to the impact of the trauma of abuse.

When I turned 50, I stopped caring about what people thought. I was 50 and free. Going through menopause really opened my eyes to a lot of things; like, I was still living my life for other people and playing too small. So, in 2019, I decided that I would no longer play small. I thought, 'I'm now on the other side. I have to start living my life for me now and pursuing my own dreams and deciding my direction.' That turning point was a massive wake-up call and a catalytic moment. I started to do well in everything that I attempted. Now I feel that I'm in that place of abundance, and in the last 12 months, my business has had the best revenue in a very long time. My faith is powered up. So I'm really pleased with the transition. I made my mind up that I was taking control, and nothing was going to stop me.

Claudia: Well done, Netty. Life begins at 50! There must have been particular resources that were crucial to your success. What were they?

Netty: I strongly believe in God, and without my faith, I'd probably be in a psychiatric hospital. The support of my family and close friends, great mentors, and spiritual leaders has been pivotal, too. I also work closely with my daughter—we are a very tight-knit, supportive family.

My determination has been crucial, too. Having made up my mind to press forward and grab what I know is mine has helped. So it's having that unshakable belief in where my future needs to be, alongside my age, of course, because I'm not getting any younger. The combination of the two has really given me a boot up the bum to accepting that this is my time now.

Claudia: Doing what you do involves leadership. What do you understand by leadership?

Netty: To be a good leader, you need the heart of a servant because leadership is about serving. It's also about motivating and taking people with you. Leadership in business is about building and promoting a collaborative, engaged, and informed workforce. And, if you lead by example, both ahead and alongside your staff, people are more likely to follow. There must be a demarcation, of course, but people need to see that you're not untouchable and that they can follow you.

Good leaders constantly upgrade themselves, so they learn and grow. They are self-leaders. They have self-direction, too. I don't need anyone to push me to learn—I love learning. I love developing myself, so I am equipped to lead people who work alongside me and pass on the best and most up-to-date knowledge.

Good leaders have good communication and people skills, which are really crucial for getting along with and influencing people. I love the book *How to Win Friends and Influence People* by Dale Carnegie. It speaks volumes about leadership as well. Again, it's all about trust, respect, rapport, and spirit. I think all of those things make really good leaders. Then you need to be self-aware so that you can manage how you affect others. And you need to be aware of your staff and their needs to get the best out of them. Again, you need practical, tactical skills, process skills, effective planning skills, and the ability to define clear performance objectives. You also need analysis and problem-solving skills, all the things that are required to be a solution carrier rather than a problem creator. A good leader is accountable to a coach or a mentor, someone who helps them to do what they are supposed to do to stay on the right track or change course when necessary. I would highly recommend having a coach or a mentor.

Claudia: How has your view of leadership informed your role as a black woman who is a leader?

Netty: It was challenging leading my business in the earlier years. I would work alongside organisations that were mainly white male-dominated. I've been in meetings where I'm the only woman and the only black person in the room. You sit at the table, and you notice who is around it, not that you're looking for that, but you automatically notice your difference. My natural response is to automatically feel that I have to stand taller than the other parties around the table, not necessarily because they have an issue with difference, but because of my makeup due to how life has been for us as black people. We are talking about 400 years or so of having to fight for our own independence and our rights. And being a woman brings another layer of oppression.

I've worked with police forces where there is known to be a lot of discrimination. Sometimes I'm there thinking, 'Who am I?' but also, 'Thank God that I'm here to work with them.' I have to be that change I want to see wherever I work. I have to stand up and stand out for those without a voice. That is why I love restorative justice because it gives a voice to the harmed.

So, as a black woman, you need to have a very strong character to be able to enter into those types of domains. You need to really know your stuff, be confident in your role, and remain unthreatened by politics and any underhandedness.

As a black woman, I bring my unique perspective on race and hate crime as well as my life experiences to the role. I've been involved in situations similar to that of some of my clients, particularly those who have been victims of domestic abuse and hate crime. But, because I'm a woman on the other side who's been elevated from that position of victim, they don't know that I've a story they can relate to until I open my mouth. So being a black woman with my particular perspective and personal experience carries influence.

Being a black woman and a leader in my numerous roles has been a strength. Organisations like the police, whom I've trained, have embraced me and my expertise. I've also played a huge role as an active influencer in Christian and community pastoring.

Claudia: So, thinking about your experience as a leader, what top three tips would you give to women of colour who want to be leaders in their field?

Netty: First, be confident in who you are. That means getting to know yourself well and showing up with confidence. You'll be able to stand up and present your subject and yourself as a leader with authority, and you'll be clear on why people should listen to you and follow you. You're fighting male dominance and the cultural and racial aspects from the start. As a woman of colour, you've got to fight even harder because of how other people regard both your race and gender. So confidence is crucial for getting through that fight.

To develop confidence, empower yourself through personal development, and mix with like-minded women. Find a mentor to support you and help you to grow and progress. And find good role models in women who are already doing what you're doing because you can learn from those that had gone before you and paved the way.

Second, be comfortable in your own skin—don't see gender or colour as barriers. See them as tools you can use to give you your unique perspectives and help other people to learn from your experiences. You have to be strong enough to handle what will come, because it's a dog-eat-dog world out there, and the higher you go, the harder it gets, especially in a male-dominated environment.

It helps to read, watch, and listen to personal development techniques such as positive affirmations. My faith and my belief in God keep me going because my perspective of who I am now comes from a divine place rather than one of vulnerability or uncertainty. If you don't have a God perspective, then connect with a higher source than yourself, the spirit perhaps, or people who will empower you to be the best version of yourself.

Third, keep yourself well-versed and educated—research, research, research. The world is always changing, and you've got to stay at the top of your game. So keep learning and developing. Know the current trends in your industry, or you'll stagnate, and your business will suffer. Ensure that you've always got something fresh to say. That's how I got involved in restorative justice. No one else was offering it locally, so I was ahead of the game. I became the go-to person for restorative justice service delivery and training in my part of the world.

You'll be able to go into environments and say something new and relevant because people will regard you as an expert, and you'll be called on to speak on your topic. I've been on BBC radio and television several times because I'm seen as an expert. It keeps you in the mind of industry leaders.

Keeping yourself knowledgeable and educated involves being prepared for any eventuality, because life can sometimes take a turn that we don't expect. For example, we are currently dealing with a global pandemic that none of us expected to land on our doorstep.

So, as a woman, and as a woman of colour, because that's what we're specifically talking about—what resources can we identify that we can lean on to make sure that our businesses, our financial status, and our families stay afloat?

And remember that, as people of colour, we've had to get ourselves well-educated because we've needed to be twice as good as our white counterparts to get on. We have to prove our worth to the outside world and sometimes to ourselves. With so many barriers to get over, being well-educated is a way of getting ahead with all the competition around us.

And a fourth tip is that, in times of chaos and uncertainty, we have to be adaptable because we may need to adjust and change direction. And that may mean putting down something that we've done for years and picking up something fresh and new. Now, that might seem scary, but, actually, when you're doing something new, you'll probably realise that that is the pathway designed for you. Because you are connected to spirit or God, and you understand your true calling and purpose. That's my belief.

You will know that you've found your calling when you become someone that other women are looking up to. I might not be an Oprah, but I was nominated for a global award last year for the outstanding work I'm doing. So being celebrated by other women of colour helps us to realise that we have power as black women, which needs to be celebrated. That's what it did for me. It showed me that I was on the right track, and it pushed me to keep on going. It's almost as if it has given me the fuel for my petrol tank that sometimes runs on empty.

I get younger girls wanting me to mentor them in life, money, and business. And I feel very honoured to be able to share my wisdom, my expertise, my knowledge, my failings, my first attempts at learning with the black women of the next generation. Because that's really what life is about; I didn't do it right the first time, but you can learn from my experiences and get there quicker than I did.

'It's crucial that women especially have the capacity and know-how to create their own economy so that they can do more, get back to their families, and serve in the community they have been called to. That way, they are able to leave legacies for their children as well.'

— Netty

CHAPTER 9

Marsha: The Young Women's Development Leader

It's interesting that 66.6 per cent of Britons support gender equality, yet only 7 per cent dare to call themselves feminists. Why the discrepancy? When feminists are stereotyped as man-hating, bra-burning, angry, hairy and dull, it's hardly surprising that so many people—this Page 1 Woman included—shy away from identifying as feminists. She's a big supporter of gender equality, and her business is about the empowerment of girls and young women, but... '*I don't call myself a feminist, although I wholeheartedly believe in equality,*' she said. '*I just don't do name tags.*'

She's Marsha Powell, leader of BelEve UK and a silver winner for Charity Champion 2021 at the Best Business Women Awards. She's the woman who, as a girl, dreamt about working in Canary Wharf and, above all, achieved it. The woman who joined the Financial Services Authority (FSA) as a teenager and broke the mould by jumping from administrator to HR business partner amidst a world full of doubts. She gathered a batch of qualifications along the way while working full-time and raising her two children.

'*People were like, 'How did you do that?' It was about achieving something for me and my children,*' she said, '*and showing them that anything is possible, even as a black girl from South East London.*'

How did she do it? Faith. Marsha is a spiritual woman, brought up in the church. Even in this era of turbulence, the Black Lives Matter movement, global warming and a worldwide coronavirus pandemic, Marsha feels she has thrived because of her faith. She's a bold, enthusiastic, and positive being, inspired by her mom. She's a self-leading free spirit who has proven that she's able to achieve anything she puts her mind to. Her business is her life purpose, her way of serving, making a difference, and paying it forward.

Let's meet Marsha Powell…

THE INTERVIEW

Claudia: Describe your work, Marsha.

Marsha: My family-run business, BelEve UK, supports girls and young women aged 8 to 21 to realise their dreams and gain the capability to increase their life chances and career prospects. If you don't have the right skills at the right time with the right type of experience, then your possibilities are reduced. Now the question is, 'What is 'right?' And the answer remains, 'Whatever is right for you.'

We aim to inspire, empower, build confidence and the moral compass of young girls before they are fully influenced by the wildness of our world. Nowadays, what social media tells you is right and wrong may not be aligned with the best values. That's why we start with eight-year-olds because we can instil values that align with what the world actually wants. And that's not about building robots. That's about enabling girls who don't have classical music playing in the background at home every day to understand that success is determined by you. And to be successful, you need to have core capabilities, such as communication, teamwork, self-leading, and good relationship-building. Even eight-year-olds can have dreams. Using myself as a good example, when I was eight, I would look outside my bedroom window and stare at Canary Wharf Tower. I didn't realise that my dream was to be there until I actually got to work there and remembered being fascinated by that tower as a child. So it's about ensuring that we support girls in building their dreams by giving them new experiences and opportunities. If we do it early, then the possibilities for these girls will become greater and better.

We work predominantly with corporates to deliver some of our work. Every half-term, we have a career insight day within a particular industry for 30 girls between the ages of 14 and 18. They do a couple of challenges, and then we give five girls, who are assessed throughout the day, the opportunity to have work experience. We've partnered with a number of companies, such as The Albany Theatre, Bloom UK, TikTok and BMW, Park Lane.

We reach some of our girls through our work in schools in the London borough of Lewisham. And we run events across London for moms and daughters and families, which brings us into contact with these girls. We create a fun, non-threatening, non-judgmental environment with clear ground rules and boundaries that's like a mini world. We use social media platforms such as Facebook, Twitter, and Instagram to market ourselves and attract people.

We also do a lot to develop their leadership capabilities so that these girls can lead their own world and recognise the qualities needed to lead themselves well. Qualities such as understanding who you are and why you are here—something we hardly talk about in this society. You need to fully understand what self-love is, too. We aren't taught to love ourselves first before seeking love from other people. So it's not the traditional leadership capabilities; it's more about self and being truly honest and open with yourself.

Claudia: Setting up and running a successful business is no mean feat. What essential steps did you take to get to where you are today?

Marsha: My first essential step was studying people. I'm an observer, and if I want to engage in something, I use my intuition and find someone who has done or is doing that same thing with great expertise and authenticity, and then mirror what they're doing. Being very curious, I would study people whom I saw as successful. I would ask, *'Does this person inspire me?'* And if yes, I would speak to them, learn more about them, and role model them.

I joined the FSA as an administrator when I was 19, with a few GCSEs. Staying as an administrator wasn't an option for me. I'm not downplaying the role because I think administrators play a huge part in any organisation. The FSA was an organisation with well-educated middle-class people, and I realised that education and putting learning into action was everything. People say it's not, but it is. I thought, *'If I'm going to get on in this organisation, I need to get myself educated because they only respect education here.'* So I had to step up and say to my line manager, 'I want to go back to college to do a business course.' She said, 'But how's that going to support you in your job?' And I had to think, 'I work in a business, right? Well, how am I going to be the best person in the business if I don't understand business?' Her mouth had dropped, and she was like, 'Okay, Marsha, you can go back to college.' That was me being bold. None of the administrators could believe that I had been bold enough to say that to my line manager and get to go back to college. That was the first incident of me being bold in the workplace and getting what I wanted. And it propelled me on because I became known for speaking out, especially for the right things. They liked me for that.

So I did a Higher National Diploma in Business Studies, followed by a degree, and then my master's in personal development. Alongside all of these, I had two kids and worked full-time. People would always ask, 'How did you do that?' But it was about me achieving something for myself and my children and showing them that anything is possible. Because what were my possibilities? My possibilities were young, black girl from Turnham in Brockley, and everything that comes with that. And then I'm 19, at the FSA, the UK's financial regulators, and I'm making moves. I'm being respected. I'm in the canteen, and people are asking, 'Who is that?'

I broke barriers at the FSA when I became the only black HR business partner[18] who got promoted from administrator. They all said, 'You can't jump from administrator to HR business partner. It's too big a leap.' I was like, 'Okay, watch me.' And, yes, I did it.

I also set up the first Black and Minority Ethnic network within the FSA. They asked me to set it up and lead its affairs. It's a matter of breaking barriers. I can walk away, and say, 'I did that'—not solely by myself, but I was chosen to lead it in an organisation of over 3,000 employees.

All those achievements show that anything is possible. It's about alignment. Alignment with yourself. Alignment with your Higher Being because I've had tough times when I had to come home and pray. Plus, alignment with truth. You know, I was never anything peculiar but Marsha at FSA, and I never ever did anything that was outside my moral code. And I received more in abundance.

---

18 HR business partners work with teams, managers, and key stakeholders to help build organisation and people capability, and shape and implement effective people strategies and activities within the organisation. https://www.cipd. co.uk/careers/career-options/hr-business-partner-roles#gref

Another essential step was to always have a plan in my working life. In 15 years at the FSA, I always had a plan that ensured I got as much as I gave. Every time I reached a milestone, I created another plan, which wasn't necessarily a physical plan, but maybe a plan in my head—what's next? We have to keep asking ourselves challenging questions, and we have to be clear on what's next. When I realised that I was no longer getting what I needed at the FSA, that's when I left.

Networking and growing my network have also been essential. The statement, 'Your network is your net worth', is so true. Using BelEve as a good example, during the last seven years, I've been able to extend my network outside the corporate environment. It's enabled me to propel my organisation forward because I keep meeting diverse people who are successful in different areas of the workplace or society. This has helped me to open myself up to different perspectives. A lot of the time, I get favours from not just people I know directly, but people I know indirectly, too. So someone in my network will say, 'Oh, you want to do that? Okay, I know this person who can help.' So I think your ecosystem is so, so important. As people of colour, we're only just realising how powerful having a solid network is. When I was at work, I used to always wonder why people took 10 minutes to have a cup of tea and a chat when they had work to do. But it's just that we need to connect. I need to know what I don't know, and I know that you know. So let me sit down with you for 10 to 15 minutes and find out over a cup of tea.

Here's a good example of the power of networking: Sister Snog, a club for businesswomen. My joining in 2016 was one of the best things that I'd ever done. Annie and Hela, the founders, have created a phenomenal sisterhood. The women who go there know how to support each other. I don't think any of them do much business outside of Sister Snog. So all the money gets circled around the club. For example, if I need a photographer, an accountant, a lawyer, or a marketer, I can find them all in Sister Snog. We build each other up and have fun together. I mean belly laugh fun. Every first Friday, we go to lunch, eat a lot of food, discuss a couple of questions, and have a good laugh. So, literally, you're just growing and excelling with this bunch of women. Most of them are white women. But that has never been a barrier for me because I'm confident, and I always know what I'm bringing to a party. There's no conversation anyone can have with me, and I look like I'm lost. I've made certain that I'm knowledgeable so that I can hold my own in any conversation.

Claudia: I just love your confidence, Marsha. Brilliant! So what was the most significant thing that got you into your current position?

Marsha: The most significant thing was the death of my mom. She was diagnosed with cancer, and 10 weeks later, she was gone. But it was the best 10 weeks of her life, I'm sure. I literally put down all my tools and moved back home. I watched her, with grace, manage her journey with courage—still giving, loving, knowing that she was going to another place.

I remember the day they said that my mom had just three months left, and at that point, she actually had two weeks. And we came home, and I said, 'Are you okay, Mommy?' She said, 'Yeah.' I said, 'You can't be okay because I'm not okay.' She said, 'You know what? The only thing I'm worried about are my daughters. Marsha, you're tough. I need you to be tough and make things happen. Everything I taught you, Marsha, I want you to put on your big drawers and show people exactly who I've created.' And I was like, 'Okay. I'll put on my big drawers, and let's make this party happen.'

The day my mom died was the first day me and my sisters left the house to get our hair done. We got a call from the hairdressers to come home. She died before we arrived and willed herself back because there was no way she wanted to die without us present. Within half an hour of us getting back, my mom died in my arms. That experience was surreal, my turning point. It made me understand how important life is and how quickly it can vanish—sometimes before you even expect it.

When my mom died, I made a big decision. I decided to live with 'I did' rather than 'I wish'. Not long before she died, I remember her saying, 'I've had 52 fantastic years. I've loved my life.' And I thought, 'I'm going to start loving my life, too. I'm going to stop looking at the things that haven't happened and look at the things that have and will happen as a result of me putting on those big drawers.' Within a year of my mom dying, I gave up my job. My big drawers have given me confidence. They help me to do absolutely anything.

Wearing your big drawers is about believing in yourself and wearing your confidence to enable you to do absolutely anything that you desire. My mom was the fifth of nine children, the last daughter and the most courageous, the most loved, the most... I don't know. I believe she was an angel. And what I did was study my mom in her final eight weeks.

When we buried her that Saturday, over a thousand people came to the funeral. When I stood up with my sisters to do the eulogy, and I suddenly saw how many people were in that church, I was like, 'I'm Delores Diana Hay's daughter. I've got to put on those drawers she talked about. I've got to, in her name. She will not die in vain.' I still wear them. I'm wearing them today.

It's so important to believe in yourself and what you're doing. A lot of people get stuck because they're comparing themselves to other people. I'd never done anything like BelEve before. I'd never run a business, although I had a business degree. I entered a market and a sector that I had never ever been part of. I could have become stuck. I could have gotten nowhere. But I knew what I wanted to do, and I went for it. I believe in what I'm doing. But that confidence and self-belief obviously were developed over time. I just think if you don't believe in yourself, no one ever will. Self-belief and passion are at the root of my success. Three years ago, we became a charity. I reached a point where I couldn't drive things anymore by myself. I needed help. So I now have a board of trustees, whereas before, we were doing it by ourselves, and we didn't ask for help. Now we have another five women on our board who support us, and it's been absolutely amazing.

Claudia: Life is obviously full of challenges; working at the FSA and setting up a business have had their challenges. What were the greatest challenges that you faced as a black woman on your journey?

Marsha: One of my greatest challenges was losing my mom. But it led me to leave my job, which was the boldest decision I've ever made. I had two children, two mortgages, and a big car. And when

I said I was leaving, people were, 'How are you going to make money?' And I said, 'Faith will guide me, lead me, and provide for me.' And at that point, I said to myself, 'Okay, Mom's not here, but spiritually she'll always be with me. So let's take this step in faith and do it.' I went ahead and set up the business, and eight years on, I'm still able to pay my mortgage. I allowed my prayers and my faith to determine my decisions. Although setting up BelEve UK put me totally outside my comfort zone, I knew my purpose and my vision, and I used all my transferable skills to make it happen.

Another big challenge came before any of this. It came when I started at the FSA as an administrator. I got stereotyped and experienced lots of micro-aggression. For example, I went into work one day wearing a pencil skirt, and my white colleague was wearing exactly the same skirt, too. My white manager pulled me to one side and said, 'Marsha, you can't wear that skirt to work; it's too revealing.' So I said, 'Jane, what are you talking about? I'm wearing the same skirt as Rebecca, and you've said nothing to her. It sounds a little bit like discrimination.' But imagine if I wasn't confident—I would have gone back to my seat and started to doubt myself, my body image, my whole being in the workplace. Obviously, when you go to work, you need to be professionally dressed, and I was professionally dressed.

Her problem was my big bum. It was a pencil skirt which was below my knee. So the only thing that she was talking about was how the skirt fit me versus my colleague. But I'm a black woman, and black women are curvy. You can't tell me that I can't wear a pencil skirt which is normal work attire. I think that incident made her understand who Marsha Powell was. I was like, 'Nah, come on, Jane. You can't say that to me. That's not right. I've got the same skirt on as Rebecca.'

I've had people telling me that I've got a chip on my shoulder because I've called someone out for unacceptable behaviour, or because I've said something that everyone else wants to say but didn't. Call me outspoken or assertive, because I am. But a chip on my shoulder? You can't say I've got a chip on my shoulder. I was also told by a person who offered me a job that they thought I was bolshie. She said, 'I feel really bad because I thought you were really bolshie. But when I saw you in the interview, I thought, 'Oh my God, what an amazing young woman.' I turned to her and said, 'You know, I've never ever had a conversation with you. So did you make that judgement based on seeing me in the canteen putting my money in the slot machine?' She went red. I was labelled bolshie just because I was going to work with confidence and nice hair, wearing heels, and pretty clothes. Another stereotype. This stuff causes people to make judgements about us, and they make decisions based on those judgements.

I've seen it in HR. I've seen it when they're deciding how much to pay people whilst they make judgments based on people's skin colour. Even though they try to be covert, as a person of colour, you know what they're doing because it's not the first time it's happened to you. But the problem for my divisions at the FSA was me being a woman of colour. So they needed to justify why they were paying me x, y, and z, even though I was doing the same job as the white person on a higher salary.

I've addressed all of this stuff by just being Marsha. I'm outspoken, but I don't speak out unless I've got something important to say. And I don't add to a part unless it is valid or I'm adding value. Also, I made sure I got myself educated. So, during my last year at work, I had a bunch of heads of department telling me that I know nothing about HR. And I've got a masters! Once I told them that I had a masters, they looked at me very differently. So I've had to be tactical.

I applied for a job as an HR business partner and was told that I wasn't quite ready. 'You've got the qualifications, and you've got the theory, but you've not got the practical experience,' they said. I told them, 'That's funny because my manager was sick for three months and I had to step up for her. She was happy for me to step up, and it worked out well. But now you're saying you're not going to give me the same job I stepped up to. Okay, cool, no problem.' So I applied for another job in another department, and I got it. And all of a sudden, I was ready. Those same people who told me that I wasn't ready then offered me the first job. I said, 'Oh, I thought I wasn't ready. Interesting.' I accepted the original role as it was my dream job.

You can't fight fire with fire. This is something I learned. If you understand the game and understand the systems in the game, you're always going to win. During my last year at the FSA, my manager said that, for my appraisal, I was a 'one', which meant that I was underperforming. The year before, I was a 'three', which was overperforming. She asked me to sign my appraisal. I said, 'What appraisal? You mean the one that says I'm a "one" and underperforming?' I said, 'No. I don't agree with anything that you've written about me. An appraisal is supposed to be a conversation, and we've not had that conversation. You've not given timely feedback to support the narrative that is in my appraisal.' I did not sign that document.

Now, as a black woman running BelEve, I can't pinpoint a time when I experienced discrimination because of my colour. But there again, I'm operating from a higher status. I'm doing a lot of driving. And I go into arenas where I believe I'm going to succeed. Whereas when you're in a system like the FSA, you have to navigate that system. But when you create the system, you do so according to your own rules. However, alongside BelEve, I run a studio in Battersea, and in that role, I've had loads of encounters with people of no colour who have tried it on with me. But it's how you respond that matters. Sometimes people want to attack you, perhaps because they feel they can, or maybe they don't respect you because they've never come in contact with anyone like you. So, for example, Meghan Markle. The British public had never seen a woman of colour like Meghan with her own people in the royal family. The fact that her mom is black with dreadlocks and a nose ring—it's like, what the hell are you bringing into our royal family? It's like, 'Nah, you're diluting our royalty.' In everything, I'm able to self-regulate by stepping back and giving a conscious response to negativity rather than a quick reaction. And when you fully understand who you are and what you bring to the party, you never ever have to react from a negative place.

Claudia: A journey such as yours is likely to have generated lightbulb moments. What was your greatest lightbulb moment?

Marsha: My greatest lightbulb moment happened at my mom's funeral when I stood to do the eulogy. I saw about 1,000 people packed into a church for 500. There were people in the aisles standing; there were people at the front standing. And, suddenly, I was facing this sea of people, all there to celebrate her life. It was thrilling. They confirmed my belief that she was an angel. She wasn't a celebrity, but a good person who touched many people's lives. She would go to the bus stop and make a new friend. Who does that?

Standing in front of all those faces doing that eulogy, I learned that I've got a purpose and a responsibility to myself, my children, and the world. The lightbulb moment was that life is about legacy and living a good life. What are you going to leave behind? What impact are you going to have on your friends, your family, the world in general? And who are you going to be while you are still here? And fast forward to five years later, I realised that I was on my journey to grace, that state of truth, happiness, forgiveness, peace. It's a journey to oneness. I believe that we're all searching for the same things: truth, love, happiness, peace, and forgiveness. For me, that's grace. When you find those things within yourself, you've got grace. I think I'm at the point of having a level of consciousness. I've recently become awakened; I see life differently, and I attend to life differently. So those things that used to really get on my nerves I let go because I'm always asking myself, 'What is the greater good in this?'

Claudia: Your mom was a great resource for you in terms of what she taught you and her encouragement. And you would have other resources that sustained you. Was there one resource that was crucial to your success?

Marsha: My faith and spirituality have been essential to my success. I remember going to church at Easter, and my pastor said, '*Faith has no sense. You can't touch, feel, or see it, but you just know it.*' So I use my intuition a lot, and when I don't use my intuition, that's when things go wrong. So I listen to my 'her', my spirit, and I allow it to guide me. Things go wrong when I don't listen.

Tuning into my faith and spirituality has enabled me to see things for what they are. I'll give you a really good example. I said to a friend, '*I've got tickets, we're going out.*' She replied, '*I'm busy.*' I was so upset, but I had to tell myself, '*You're transferring negative energy into the atmosphere.*' I had to get myself out of it because I'm in control of my feelings and my state— mentally, spiritually and physically. When people realise they have self-control, we won't have a world of confusion.

Another resource that has contributed to my success is my strong sister unit. My three sisters and I are really close. We support each other and complement each other. If one of us lacks expertise, one of the others will definitely have it. Two of my sisters work for me now; that's why it's a family business. We work really well as a unit.

Claudia: Let's talk about leadership because leading is what you've been doing, isn't it? What do you understand by leadership?

Marsha: Leadership is about leading yourself and others authentically towards a vision and a purpose whilst being conscious of what and who you put out there. Leadership is about bringing people along with you and listening to their views. So sometimes, your vision isn't the one that's going to get you to where you want to be. But you can never know everything. So a leader has to be open to learning from others. Sometimes I learn from my children because they teach me things that make me a better person. So they enable me to lead myself better.

Claudia: What do you bring to the leadership role as a woman leader?

Marsha: Men are very bottom-line driven, whereas women leaders often consider the people before the numbers and *how* we did and not *what* we did. So, men and women look at things from different perspectives. We may get to the same place but in different ways.

I think of myself more as a leader rather than a woman leader. What makes me who I am is my spirit and being human. I focus on why I'm here rather than the label and restrictions that have been put on me, specifically because I'm a woman. Let me live a free-spirited life as Marsha Powell, a human being, here to support women to realise their dreams.

I chose to work with girls and young women as I'm a fantastic human being because my mom was my cheerleader. Loads of girls don't have that. I wanted to recreate some of the gems my mom gave me and give back to society. As women, we're powerful. The world tells us we're secondary, that men rule, make the big decisions, are successful, and have more money. So we feed into that theory and don't realise our power. Women are the world's creators. No babies, no world. But we can't do it without the men. We can only do it together.

Claudia: How would you say your view of leadership has informed your role as a leader who happens to be a black woman?

Marsha: Do you know what? I just think everyone is a leader, but I think when you are not even just a black woman but a black person, you always have to make sure that you double down on yourself. You have to make sure all of your 'T's and your 'I's are crossed and dotted because even if just one isn't, someone could see it as an opportunity to discredit you and your hard work. I think that we are always trying to prove that we should be sitting at that leadership table, which is oftentimes created by others. And that can be exhausting at times. What's beautiful is that, as people of colour, we are now saying, 'No—actually, I don't need to be at that table; I can create my own.'

Someone who has recently made me think is P Diddy. He's like, 'Coronavirus is here, and we've got a problem. And the problem is that black people are dying more than any other race. We can either hear it and do nothing about it, or we can do something about it. Our health carers haven't got the right uniforms, PPE, blah, blah, blah. We can talk about it, or we can do something about it. First things first, I've got a platform where we can talk about it. It's my platform. So, ownership. We can say what we want to say.' So Diddy has a debate with all the influential people that he believes should be at the table, and they talk about not just the problem, but what the solutions are. Then he has a dance-a-thon, and he raises $4m. Then he says that every day at 5:00 'We're going to have black news. We're going to talk about the good things that happen in the black community because we need to hear more of these things because what we hear on the TV is not our news—it's all negative.' And when they want us to speak, do you know what they do? They cut us off when we get to the bit that's passionate. So, we need to avoid getting into positions where we're always having conversations about ourselves as disempowered victims. We need to create our own conversations and bring our own along with us. Because white people bring their own along with them, Indians bring their own along with them. It's like, I'm going to go for the door, and although I can't bring everyone through, once I'm through it, I'm going to come back for you. But, in our Caribbean culture, it's about you got rich and switched. And no, I can't put you on my back when my back is not strong.

My children's dad is Ghanaian, so I've experienced the Ghanaian community. If one of them says, 'We're doing this,' they all come together to bring it to fruition. But there again, where black Caribbean people start from is different from where black Africans start. Because those in Africa didn't become slaves, so they have a different mentality. And I believe they don't have the trauma of slavery in their DNA. How do we, as descendants of slaves, break that chain? We have to do it consciously; by transforming our mentality and our mindset.

When we look at America, I know it's a huge place, but we see many successful black people there. Whereas, in the UK, you don't see successful black people without consciously searching for them—outside of football and music, to be precise. We see successful black Americans every day. We know them. Our children know them. That shows us that it can be done. The question is, what's behind it? What I see is a community. That's what I see in America. Whereas I don't see that here in the UK. You know, if P. Diddy says he's doing something, they all get on board. And yeah, he's got money, I understand that. But you see those BET awards, black Americans come out and show up. Tyler Perry does his thing, and the community shows up. And some people might see that as far-reaching, but is it? No, it isn't. It's about mentality and mindset.

Why do we need validation? Why do we need acceptance from anyone other than ourselves? If Africa is the richest continent, why are we not ensuring that it reaps from the riches of Africa? Because everything they need, they already have. So why do I go there and see poor, poor people when all the riches are there? Again, it's about mentality and our ability to believe that we can stand on our own two feet. As black women, we must do our bit for each other as much as for everyone else. That means that my charity will benefit from you. So sometimes, we just need to be clear on what our game plan is and the pieces we need to be successful with our game.

Claudia: Yes, we absolutely should be supporting each other. So, what three top tips would you give to women of colour who want to be leaders in their field?

Marsha: I would say lead consciously. I've read *The Conscious Leader* by Labek Watson. So, my first tip is to consciously lead myself and others towards a vision. When you do, you get to live in and enjoy the moment with the people who matter.

Second, always serve, and make that your first premise. Pay it forward. Good leaders understand the power of giving. When you give, you get plenty back. Always consider who you're empowering and inspiring. You'll get self-fulfilment, confirmation that you're doing what you set out to do, and that you're passing it on. And that's about serving, leading with excellence, and being the best person you can be in any position.

Serving gives you the ability to continue to serve. Because when you understand that serving is a continuous thing, you'll see it as a way of life. I went to church once, and a rabbi came and said, *'Jews are so successful because their first principle is to serve. So we get back in abundance.'* If every day you think, *'What am I going to give to the world and those around me?'* you'll receive back amply.

Since paying it forward with BelEve UK, I've got peace, happiness, truth, and love. I wake up each morning and determine my day. At the centres, I have girls and young women happy to see me because of what we've given them. So, paying it forward enables another individual to understand love, truth, forgiveness, peace—all the things we adults seek.

Finally, always make sure that you're an expert in your particular field. Because, as black women, we're always having to prove ourselves. If that one thing that you know is your thing, no one can take that away from you. All the successful black women that I know are specialists, experts in a particular field. It's not enough to be a generalist. No one respects that because you're a woman with many coats. But if you're a specialist, people respect and honour it. You are the go-to person. They want to know what you know. I have a friend who is an expert in joy. And do you know what? She has women who just want to hear what she's got to say about joy. How beautiful is that? Specialising in that way gives you fulfilment.

At the end of the day, why are we here? If we're not wholeheartedly enjoying standing upon the earth that God has given us, why are we here? If today you aren't living a fulfilled life, are you working towards it? And if you're not, why not? That would be my thing. You know, this is the happiest I have ever been in my life, although my mom is not on this earth. So, why? Because I have freedom. I get up in the morning, and I decide what I'm doing. And because I know something, I can dip in and dip out. So many opportunities come my way on LinkedIn. Every now and again, I just post something about my specialty and let people know what I'm doing. And I continue to build my network and add value.

'Being very curious, I would study people whom I saw as success-ful. I would ask, 'Does this person inspire me?' And if yes, I would speak to them, learn more about them, and role model them.'

— Marsha

CHAPTER 10

Razia: The Affordable Housing Campaigner

Now here's an interesting figure: circa 200,000 people in England experienced homelessness in 2020.[19] Bear in mind that that figure doesn't include those experiencing inadequate and overcrowded housing conditions.

With affordable housing in London out of reach for a significant number of people, what are the chances of getting adequate accommodation when you're on an average wage? If you're an above-average earner, or you can rely on the coffers of mum and dad to bail you out, you're ok, right? But throw race inequality into the mix, and you find that global majority communities are:

- 'Over-represented in insecure private rented sector accommodation;
- More likely to be overcrowded and experience poor housing conditions impacting health;
- Three times more likely to be over-represented in the most deprived local authority areas; and,
- Three times more likely than white households to experience homelessness.' [20]

This is the predicament faced by thousands of people in 21st century London.

Now picture this: you are a successful career woman, married with two growing kids. You need more space and to remain near your supportive, extended family. But, as years roll by, you witness

19 Crisis
20 Abdul A Ravat; Vice-Chair, Manningham Housing Association

the area transform——shifting demographics and house prices way beyond your average pay scale. Frustrating, right? So what do you do?

This was the reality that propelled my Page 1 Woman Razia Khanom, to set out on an extraordinary journey: from sceptical mum seeking an affordable family home to passionate campaigner for decent, inexpensive housing for below-average earners. And it happened unexpectedly, in a way she couldn't have predicted or believed. If someone had told her how things would pan out, she might have responded, 'Shut the front door——pronto!'

Razia Khanom is a politically-savvy problem-solver, a determined, committed, forthright woman who got off her butt and found a solution, initially for her family and later for countless others who share her dream for nothing fancy, just suitable, inexpensive, adequate homes. Along the way, her purpose expanded to serving as a role model for her daughters to demonstrate the difference that smart, courageous, clear-thinking, single-minded women of colour can make in the world. Well, be prepared to be uplifted.

THE INTERVIEW

Claudia: Tell us, Razia, what do you do?

Razia: I wear different hats for my professional career. I studied accountancy and fell into credit control and risk. My current job is an off-shoot of my career. I work in the credit control department of a newspaper publication called *First News*, a children's newspaper that's great to work for.

I'm also a cake decorator as a hobby. It's my release. More recently, as an active member of the Woman's Equality Party, I'm on its Race Equality Caucus Committee. But my real passion is not a paid job. We tend to think of work as having to be paid. But I've learned that work is something we do that benefits in some way—like being a mom, for example. It's not always paid. I'm a volunteer board member for London Community Land Trust. I co-chair its Social Impact subcommittee. Our aim is to bring genuinely affordable housing to London. By 'genuinely affordable', I mean houses that are priced below market value. They're about 60 per cent of market value so that people that live in the locality, who are on an average wage for that locality, can afford to buy a home and call it their own rather than being subjected to unscrupulous landlords. It's a charitable interest organisation that makes no profit off the back of it. So, as you can imagine, people get good 60 per cent market value homes for life. And it keeps our communities and our families together whilst maintaining diversity in the area. That's been my driving passion for the last three years.

Claudia: So, how did you get into this campaign?

Razia: Interestingly, I live in Brixton. I've lived here for 16 years now. My husband was born in Brixton, and his family lived in the area, too. Over the years, we've seen sweeping gentrification and demographic changes here. I took a career break when I had my eldest daughter, who is 11 now. My husband's grandmother raised him after his mom passed away when he was 10. So she's my children's great-grandmother. I made it my mission to make sure that my eldest daughter and her great-grandmother got to spend as much time together as possible before the inevitable. So, every week, I would pick her up from home on a Thursday morning and take her into Brixton market with me and my daughter to do the shopping. And in those few years, I saw such a drastic change in Brixton market, which was nothing short of gentrification.

As my daughter was growing up, we went from two healthy incomes to one income. I chose to become a full-time mom at home, so we knew we were going to take a big hit. But the country went into recession around that time, and I had to go back to work, and it wasn't easy. When I was job hunting, often, as soon as employers knew that you had a young child or it was assumed you were of childbearing age, they didn't want to risk taking you on. I was once being interviewed, and I noticed the face drop of one of the interviewers when they noticed that my belly was a little bigger than it really should be. That's when I kind of thought, 'I can't put my finger on it, but I know what's going on here.'

As time passed, my husband and I realised that we couldn't afford to continue living in the area we call home. So we started to talk about leaving Brixton. The cost of living had increased, but our salaries hadn't increased in line with it. So, as you can imagine, that gap between being able to afford a home and living was becoming much wider given our family's expansion. Relocating seemed to be our only option if we wanted adequate living space for our growing children.

Then, around 2018, I noticed a leaflet on our notice board, which referred to 'genuinely affordable housing'. At first, I thought it was nonsense because I knew what genuinely affordable housing looked like. Having worked for a housing association where I was an income officer, mitigating for financial risk, I witnessed affordable housing crashing down. People were buying shares in properties, and then realised that they had no prospect of owning the home because house prices were extraordinary. So housing associations lost a considerable amount of money, and I was drafted to create a robust rent collection method. But the emotional toll on me was horrendous. We were evicting families essentially so that the housing association could get more reliable tenants. That was part of the dark side of local authorities failing to invest in social and genuinely affordable housing.

So, I saw this leaflet on my notice board. Then there was a knock on the door from good old proper grassroots activists inviting us to their steering group meeting. But bearing in mind my experiences of hostility for looking like I do, I expected the meeting would be another one of those situations where I'm the only Asian woman and Muslim woman in the room. And remember, this is the height of Islamophobia, and there was hostility even in Brixton towards Muslim women.

Well, I went to that meeting anyway, and true to my expectation, I was the only Asian woman there. I sat down at the table, furthest away from everybody. It was traumatic, I realised later. Then this pastor, a lovely gentleman, came and sat next to me and introduced himself. Then this young lad also came and sat next to me. They started talking about what this actually was, and I then realised that this was the pastor for the Methodist circuit in South London. And the young gentleman who sat next to me was a member of the Youth Advocacy Academy in Stockwell. They are amazing! Amazing! The Academy is a youth-led programme. The executive is under the age of 25. The whole thing is kids leaving college going into the Youth Advocacy Academy and into politics. The application process has to be something you are angry about and what you want to do about it. That's their criteria. They are the beacon of diversity, of celebrating and valuing our youth. They are 'swear words' amazing!

So I'm there, and I'm speaking to a youth, and he explains this whole thing to me. And I realised then that this project for affordable housing was born out of the Youth Advocacy Academy. They decided that they, too, were getting tired of unaffordable housing and that they were still living with their parents. They were coming out of university and couldn't afford to call a place their home. There's no social housing available anymore. So what could they do? So they started this affordable housing campaign. They approached London Citizens, who then approached the London Community Land Trust, and they created this project called 'Christ Church Road.' They identified land that belonged to Transport for London and placed a bid for it on a small builders programme. And then we had the 'Christ Church Road' Steering Group, which I was invited to. And I sat there thinking, 'It's so tragic. When I was 17 or 18 years old, I didn't have to worry about whether there was housing.' But these kids are having to grow up so much younger because, somewhere along the line, we—generations before us and those in power—have failed them. Then I realised that this affordable housing scheme was a solution to my own housing situation.

So I'm going to these meetings, and I'm kind of quite reserved until I realise it's a safe space. I've never felt safe like this. They've got people from all different backgrounds, faith groups, no faith groups, everything, with the same collective goal to bring affordable housing to Lambeth, Brixton. It didn't matter where we were from. Most of us were probably there because we needed housing. But some of us were there because we had the tools, the power, and the organisation to make it happen. I ended up getting more involved.

There was a young lady called Leanna, one of the organisers, from the Liberal Synagogue in Streatham. She started asking me questions, and I kind of thought, 'This is really weird because there's so much cohesion here. We've got different faith groups here. We've got Muslims, Christians, Jewish, nothing, and everything going on here. And everybody is getting on amazingly well.' And I kind of got a bit suspicious: 'Why are they asking me questions? What's going on here?' They wanted to find out more about me to get me involved and representing our steering group. I had housing experience in the public and private sector and knew about legislation and how what we would be doing would be impacting people. But they recognised that I had something else, although I didn't recognise it myself. After a couple of interviews, they asked me to represent London CLT at an accountability assembly in Southwark Cathedral and pin down our politicians to make good on their tasks.

So I stood up in Southwark Cathedral, and I was nervous. It was the first day of Ramadan, and I was fasting. It was 8:00 in the evening, and I had no childcare, so my kids were with me. Then I saw my younger daughter's headteacher and deputy head there. They said they were members of London Citizens and were there to campaign against youth violence and Islamophobia. So I said, 'Fantastic! Can you look after my children? Because I'm here for the housing.' They were like, 'Yeah, fine.'

So I got up on the podium. I was so nervous, having not eaten or drunk all day. There were about 450 people in the room, and I couldn't see anything. Then, out of the corner of my eye on my right, I saw these two little monkeys come out from behind a flower stand and put their thumbs up. They were my daughters. They had heard me say I was nervous and came in to give me a vote of confidence. And then everything came into focus, on like an epiphany level focus. I thought to myself, I made that decision to quit work because I want to be able to raise my children with good values and a stable upbringing in their early years. And once they've gone into school, I can go back into doing what I do. Somewhere during that process, I had kind of lost myself. I was doing my cake decorating from home. And it dawned on me that it's all well and good choosing to be at home, raising your children, being there for them no matter what. That's fantastic, nothing wrong with it—but there is so much work to be done in society. Here I am dispelling this myth when my daughters said, 'Men are doctors, not women.' I said, 'But you've just been seen by a female pediatrician.' There I was telling my daughters there are no limits; there are no boundaries. Reach for whatever you want to reach for, yet the only female in their life was not presenting that to them. I thought, if I want them to go and take on the world, they have to see somebody take on the world. And that was it; I changed. It stopped being about a housing need for me and my family. It became about affordable housing for everyone who didn't have it.

Whilst I still believe a hundred per cent that Community Land Trust projects are the most impactful, viable, sustainable solutions to the housing crisis that we've got, I knew that I needed to spearhead this. I realised in getting involved that London CLT was aiming hard for diversity, aiming hard for equal representation. And as soon as they saw what I represented, they leapt on it and started to push me in every which direction; every manner of my discomfort zone, they sent me there. But it's been an exhilarating journey thus far. And then, sometime later, they asked me if I could make an application to become a board member as a local representative. I asked the chief executive, 'What is it about me that you want? I need to know for myself.' He said, 'You've got a unique way of telling your stories, which aren't just stories; they are your own real-life experiences. And you articulate it in a way that comes across both impactfully and emotionally. But also, it's backed up with statistics and facts, and we could do with that, especially from a local representative level. Because it's all well and good as an organisation creating homes, having the professionals, developers, contractors. But who are we building these homes for? We need somebody to be able to represent that point of view. We might create a fancy kitchen, but if we don't have parents coming in and telling us, 'Well, this sort of kitchen isn't conducive for our family life,' where can we go with it?'

It was the first time in a number of years that I finally heard someone echoing thoughts that I had in my head. And my goal now is to deliver as many homes for as many people as possible because one thing we know is that housing insecurity, job insecurity affect those from ethnic minorities first.

Claudia: Definitely. Housing and employment in the UK are rife with discrimination. But as an Asian, Muslim woman, what were the essential steps that got you to where you are now?

Razia: My biggest realisation was that to move forward, you have to stop running away from the problem and find your voice. In the Bangladeshi culture, my voice has generally been quite drowned out. Although this applies to people generally, it's more reflecting on women. One of my earliest memories is walking down the high street with my mom. There was a group of teenage white girls making fun of my mom's attire. I was livid! But my mom told me, 'Leave it. We've gone through worse than that.' I didn't know what she meant.

I used to hear stories from uncles, aunts, older relatives about the discrimination they had experienced. And then I started experiencing it myself as I got older. I had to learn that the problem wasn't mine but my aggressors. I had to overcome the mental self-doubt that crept in. I had to dare to believe in myself, evaluate my progression, recognise my talents, know when I'm being taken advantage of, and know when to challenge it. When I was younger, I had a little bit more veracity about challenging racism. Sometimes your challenge works, and at other times it doesn't. The key to moving forward is analysing the risks and recognising which fights are worth having and which won't get you far so you know when to step back and walk away. Crucially, you need to know who your allies are—whether they are white people or people like you—who you can call on for help and support in those incredibly difficult times. Like they say, 'A finger alone and a fist together.'

When you're alone in a large organisation, and you're the single voice, it's very difficult to scream louder than all those voices put together. I had to recognise where I was and how I got there. I had to get clear on my destination and the challenges I was faced with. I found like-minded people, groups, and campaigns to contribute to because there is power in numbers. I also fought with my inner doubts and fears by using affirmations and reading about campaigns people have won in the past to help increase my confidence.

Claudia: So you've clearly encountered many challenges on your journey as an Asian Muslim woman. How did you overcome them?

Razia: The primary challenge has to do with people's internal biases and assumptions. One that, as soon as I'm seen as a woman of colour, I'm somehow deemed less worthy of reward, whether that's monetary, career progression, or otherwise. You can see that in some of the places I've worked. But we also know through recent studies[21] that, as minority women, we take on a larger portion of the work burden. For example, 45 per cent of black and minority ethnic women say they have been singled out for harder or unpopular tasks at work compared to their white counterparts. And we're more likely to continue to work in the face of challenges.

I actually lost my job very early on in the pandemic and in a very sinister way. It was a part-time job in an FTSE 500 company. The most senior members of staff (director level) were female, middle management were male, and below them, there was me in a senior role. My immediate manager set a target for me, which would see him receive a massive bonus if I met the target. But he decided to set this target without telling me and then came down on me like a ton of bricks in order to achieve it. There was no structure in place at all when I joined. But he told me two months before the

---

21 BME Women and Work — TUC Equality Briefing (October 2020).

target date that I must meet this target. I point blank replied, 'We don't have the structures. It isn't going to happen.' He didn't like it. So we had this dynamic of him withholding information whilst piling more and more responsibilities on me. Then I realised that my predecessor was doing what I was doing in a full-time role. Now, I was doing full-time work and more in a part-time role.

Initially, I met the targets, as impossible as they were. Then he decided to move the goal post and set increasingly ridiculous objectives, and block my contact with other parts of the company. As an accountant, this was unworkable. We eventually parted ways, and lo and behold, three weeks later, I saw the same role advertised as a full-time position. This seemed to be about race and gender. I'd observed the interactions of my manager and the management accountant when they were dealing with their white female counterparts. Being privy to their private conversations, I noticed that my manager was inflammatory about female staff members, with aggression level increasing the darker the women's skin colour got. I approached Human Resources, a local black woman, and got my concerns across, and she developed an action plan. The next thing I knew, she had disappeared. Gone.

A lot of my family worked for the same organisation. It's the worst kept secret about their failure to invest in female members of staff. You can see this from my sister's research of the positions on the lowest rank. Black and Asian women make up over 30 per cent of their workforce in the lowest pay rank. By the time you get to a senior executive level, it goes down to less than 0.1 per cent. So it's quite evident as to who they choose to promote. Then there are the racist micro-aggressions, the comments that you get when, for example, it's prayer times, and you have to take a break to pray, or if you don't want to join when they go on a pub crawl. All of these things are looked at as if you are somehow not one of them. And some of the comments with regard to attire, for example, things like, 'Aren't you hot in that thing?' People are now more careful.

I once worked on a contract for a maternity leave cover in the accounts department of a very well-established fashion organisation. There was a young lady whose career the new financial controller wanted to help progress. I ended up having to train her around finance processes, as she had no experience of accounting and definitely no knowledge of Excel. But, because she was in a senior position, she didn't like being told that she needed a bit of training in Excel. Not easy. They kept on extending my contract. Then they decided to keep me on when the incumbent returned (as he had been on leave) but wouldn't make me permanent. And I said, 'At least let's discuss a pay rise.' They said, 'Sorry, there's nothing in the pot.' Despite the fact they had just given the woman I was training a £5,000 pay rise. And I was the one that was training her. I was the most qualified and experienced for the role, but I was the one getting absolutely nothing. I was so angry and hurt that I left. A month or two after I left, I was still getting phone calls from the woman I was training, whilst the woman I worked alongside was contacting me, too. The irony of it! They needed me, and they knew it. But, for reasons I can only put down to prejudice, they felt that the young white lady was more deserving of a pay rise than somebody who had taken on almost double the amount of work in the short time that I was there, including having to train others.

The gender and race challenges continue. When I worked for a recruitment company, I went for promotion against two male colleagues. My manager pulled me to the side and said she would love to give me the job, which she knew I could do well and even better than the two men, but because they'd been there longer, it might disgruntle them, so we're offering it to them. I said, okay that's fine. Fast forward, and I'm thinking about career progression in that company, and I realised there's no line of progression for me there. When I handed in my resignation letter, they offered me an £8,000 pay rise to stay. But I decided that it wasn't right for my career progression and left. And then, within three months, they employed two new supervisors in the same role that I'd gone for that they couldn't give me because I'd not been there long enough. But they were quite happy to recruit two men for the same role, one who would later go on to racially offend colleagues. This kind of stuff causes self-doubt, particularly when they gaslight you and try to convince you that, somehow, you're the problem.

Overcoming sometimes means that we have the advantage of being able to shout and speak out, especially in recent years. Whether people like it or not, they are forced to listen. Once upon a time, I found it easier to be totally self-reliant, so it was difficult to reach out for help. There are lots of organisations out there that have a racial/equality focus. Organisations such as the London CLT, MIND, the mental health charity, Citizens UK, and the Youth Advocacy Academy. A friend of mine runs an initiative called 'The Lantern Initiative,' which helps to tackle mental health issues—such a stigma amongst Muslim women. When you get together with fantastic women of black and Asian backgrounds, such as those in the Race Equality Caucus of the Women's Equality Party, as well as your allies, it really puts things into perspective. We learn from each other's experiences, and it allows us individually to be proactive depending on the situations we're in. It builds your confidence. It's knowing that you're not alone. And sometimes, when you're walking that really dark road alone, you know that there are loads of people facing those same challenges and that they're back there cheerleading for you. It sheds light on the path that you're on. You're able to think clearer with a bit more confidence and more self-belief. Although there is so much work to be done in challenging adverse situations that are actually challenging it rather than just going through the motions. Change is taking place.

Claudia: I'm guessing that you had numerous lightbulb moments on this amazing journey. If so, which were most significant?

Razia: Interestingly, I was working at a housing association in South London when, one day, I noticed that most of the people working there were black, African, or West Indian. It was my first experience of feeling antagonism from black people. I was really surprised… really, really surprised. One day, my husband dropped me off at work and kissed me goodbye. I was pregnant at the time. I went in, and one of my colleagues asked who he was. I was like, 'That's my husband.' He was like, 'What? You're married to a black guy?' All of a sudden, it spread like wildfire on our floor between the income officers and the housing officers, and I was welcomed into the team, into the club, after that. And that's not based on my assumption. Later, I was speaking to a lovely lady from Jamaica. She was like, 'You're one of us; you're part of the family.' I asked, 'What made me not part of the family before?' She said, 'We experience racism, not just from white people, but from Asian people, too. So we assume that everybody is racist to us until we know otherwise. And if you've married in, then you're one of us.'

It dawned on me that the hostility I'd experienced from my black colleagues was part of the trauma that they had suffered. I know that there's a huge issue of anti-blackness within Asian communities. I experienced it when I was living in East London where my husband and I met. That was one of the reasons why we chose to move down South. Now, I could have stuck my nose up at my black colleagues, and I could have said, 'Well, all of a sudden, I'm worthy of your acceptance and before, I wasn't simply because of where I'm from?' This is essentially the experience that both black and Asian people get from white supremacy. But that wasn't a fight worth having. It was an opportunity for dialogue, learning, understanding, and appreciation.

I used to talk to my husband about racism and the hostility at work. But I didn't have that dialogue within my birth family whenever I experienced racism, as I didn't recognise what it was. Growing up, I noticed the segregation in the town in which I lived, but I didn't question it because that's what I was born into. That was the norm. Moving to London, where there was so much more diversity, was such a culture shock for me. We're forced into each other's spaces here, so no segregation. So it was such a huge learning curve. Learning about my husband's experiences brought a completely different lens on things. It helped me to appreciate that what we often discuss, i.e. our experiences of being female and black, or Asian, or whatever it is, they come with different challenges. It's not a one-size-fits-all. My experiences as a Muslim Asian woman from a Bangladeshi background really did make me confront my own privileges. And with those privileges comes a responsibility to use them for the betterment of others. You don't have to be confrontational about it. But you have the opportunity to either be quiet or to use your voice to speak up against injustices. Those injustices could be ideologically based; that's generally where it begins, isn't it? So that, for me, was definitely a huge lightbulb moment.

Claudia: So we've spoken about your crucial steps, challenges, and lightbulb moment. Let's look at resources that have been crucial to your success. What were they?

Razia: As a tangible resource, I would say, other people, primarily my husband. We are two people from completely different backgrounds having lots of dialogue. Our basis is about connecting on a human level. And then, when you start breaking it down in terms of our individual experiences, it's an eye-opener for both of us. I learned about his experiences of growing up in South London and being subjected to a lot of racist stuff that I couldn't have even imagined.

I lived quite a sheltered lifestyle when growing up, which kind of helped me open up to the experiences of other people. Interestingly, when we shared experiences, we may not have been able to fully appreciate or understand them, but there was this element of solidarity. When I'm out there going about my business doing what I do, it's with an understanding of the experiences that other people have gone through, which allows me to learn and take those steps forward.

Claudia: Your current involvement in the London CLT is in a leadership role. So what do you understand by leadership?

Razia: Leadership is showing your way forward. When you lead, you're at the forefront of your fight, with other people following behind you. But you are also following in the footsteps of those who have gone before you. They may take a left or a right, but everybody's journey is their own. And leadership is generally about inspiring people to walk their journey.

My own personal preference of leadership would be to lead on an ethical basis because do you want to leave toxic fumes or a pathway behind you? You're setting precedence, whether it is for one person or 5 million people. So it's important for you to understand the responsibility that comes with that leadership. You have the onus to make sure that the legacy or the kind of inspiration that you leave behind is one of positive progression for whoever takes over from there.

Claudia: Some women leaders don't see themselves as leaders. How much do you actually see yourself as a leader?

Razia: On a scale of one to 10, 10. Everybody is a leader in their own right. I wouldn't have imagined myself as a leader five years ago. If you had told me I would be a leader someday, I would have said, 'You're having a laugh!' You just don't know which way life is going to take you. And I think everybody has talent and capability. Everybody has a positive contribution to make to society. Our contributions should mirror the best of what we can offer. And, as such, absolutely everybody is a leader. You don't have to be a grown woman to be a leader. You could be a youngster, like Greta Thunberg, and still, be a leader.

In one of my leadership roles, I've been challenging myself to be part of an organisation and a collective so that we can build a larger community, whether it's virtual or in the actual presence of each other. And everybody is part of that, so everybody leads the way there, too.

Claudia: How has your view of leadership informed your role as a leader who is a woman of colour?

Razia: I'm a co-chair of my steering group, and I'm responsible for representing the local community within my organisation. And with that, I have to always bear in mind that I'm wearing three hats at a time. I'm a woman, a person of colour, and a Muslim intersection. It's a three-way conjunction. And I'm also tasked with representing what my local community wants. So I need to be in touch with all of those elements.

I have told my board that what they are doing as an organisation, as stakeholders, and as residents is not enough because we are not moving as fast as we ought to. We wanted these homes in 2021, and we're probably not going to get them till 2023. Once upon a time, I would have been drowned out if I had taken that position. A key reason for getting involved with affordable housing and the board was that I wanted to see more people like me where I am. I want to see more black, Asian and Muslim women and everything that makes us a beautiful matriarchy. I want to see us at the forefront. We've had enough of patriarchy; it doesn't work, and that's for sure.

And I share that same mindset with our board members and our staff at the London CLT. This is what we are about, and I have a real sense of pride in that.

One of my fellow board members kind of mentored me through the process. She is amazing. I once said to her, 'You're my little personal cheerleader. When I need 'amping up' when I'm nervous, you're there constantly coaxing me on.' And she's led me, and I'm following in those footsteps. I'm adding my own flare, knowing full well that someone else is going to come up behind me. And I hope it's another woman of colour, as historically we have been told that we're either refusing to participate, or integrate or we're not as deserving. So here we are—look at us now! We're here to stay, and we're going to make waves. Basically, I'm using my identity as a leader who's a Muslim woman of colour for the good of the world.

In terms of my paid role, one of the fantastic things about where I work is that they recognise that they've got an imbalance in terms of race and gender. As soon as they get an opportunity for diverse recruitment, they lunge at it. If you see their publications! And remember, they provide a newspaper for children. I subscribed my daughter to this newspaper as part of literacy, and then, three months down the line, my friend sent me their job spec. She said, 'This might be perfect for you.' And they've got front page championing Marcus Rashford. Last year, they covered an article right on the front page of a young Somali girl in a hijab talking about how she was experiencing Islamophobia—they are really tackling it head-on. They are doing their utmost to make sure that whatever they are sending out to children in schools, whether it is through their I-Hub (their online digital package for learning), that all of this inclusive material is in there. When it comes to their recruitment policy, I've never come across an organisation like it. The vast majority of their roles are part-time, so they can have women with caring responsibilities continue to work and support their personal life. There's only one day a week on a Wednesday when every employee is technically in the office. Otherwise, everybody's roles are part-time. They make sure that women continue to have an opportunity to progress in their careers. We still have a long way to go in sharing parenting responsibilities, but this organisation is enabling that. And it doesn't come at a price, because I'm getting paid more in this job than I did at an FTSE 100 company. So I'm proud to be a part of that.

When we find allies and ally organisations, it's incumbent on us to make sure that we support them. It reminds me of a conversation that my husband and I used to have years ago. This is what really opened my eyes. We were in Brixton, where all the corner shops were owned by Asian people. I wondered, 'Where are the black businesses?' We need to recognise where we need to offer support. And we need to recognise those who are our allies. There's strength in numbers.

Claudia: So, what are your three top tips for women of colour who want to be leaders in their field?

Razia: I am going to take inspiration from H, someone in our Race Equality Caucus. I noticed that her prolonged fight against prejudice/racial inequality has started to create self-doubt about her contribution. So my first top tip is that you proactively believe in yourself. Believe in what you are doing and know that it has an impact beyond what you can possibly imagine. So don't allow self-doubt to fester. Don't let the doubt that they instil in you as a woman to take root.

When you believe in yourself, you can act with clarity and acuity, which help you affect change and lend credibility and authenticity to your cause. You aren't doing it just for yourself; you're doing it for other women of colour. But it's not just other women of colour that benefit; society at large does, too.

My next tip would be to surround yourself with good strong women of colour. They will support you. They will be your crash mat, your cheerleaders, and you absolutely deserve that. Without the support of the collective, it's quite easy to get drowned out because your voice isn't as loud as the voice of the collective. Sometimes it's quite beneficial to be in an echo chamber; it amps you up. And when you surround yourself with other strong, challenging women, they challenge you, maybe indirectly, to question and challenge yourself even further because you are capable of so much more. You're more likely to achieve your potential. And when you take inspiration from other women of colour, you'll find an amazing part of you that you didn't know existed.

I've surrounded myself with women from the Women's Equality Party's Race Equality Caucus. I'm also part of a diverse and international group of women who identify with the Muslim faith. We celebrate each other's differences and support and uplift each other. We are into eco-living because a verse in the Quran states that human consciousness has been placed on Earth as its custodian. So we're responsible for ensuring its welfare. We've got bike riding enthusiasts, and we recycle, reuse, up-cycle, ferment food—you name it.

Another thing is that mothers are primary leaders. We don't have the airs and graces of leaders or the title. But we are the primary leaders in our homes and our societies. Leaders don't need a fanfare or a title to lead. Those things are distractions. Mothers, with the right support, sure as hell make the most compassionate leaders, the most invested leaders. When it comes to moms, you're not just investing in your children; you're investing in the whole family unit and wider society. And when you look at statistics, we can all talk about gender equality till the sky turns green, but we know that women take on the mothering role, as it can only be done by women, which has far-reaching consequences. The impact is long-term—two, three generations worth. Personally, I don't think enough credit is given in that respect. I think we're living in times where value is so material and transactional that we've overlooked one of the most crucial representations of leadership in motherhood. If motherhood was recognised for what it actually is, you could put it on your CV and use examples from it of where you've led in your job interviews. If you can lead your kids in the home, you can do it anywhere—in conflict resolution, HR, business management, the whole thing. Because leading them is growing them and making them the leaders of the future.

Tip three is go for it. Go for whatever you envision in your mind. It will never be less than what it is right now. You can only achieve more. You'll probably have a whole lot of fun in the process. At worst, it will be, 'I tried, and it didn't work out,' but there will always be valuable learnings along the way. I'll put this in context for you: I was in a hospital a few years ago, and my second child was due a bit too early. It was all a bit of a rush, and I didn't know what was going on. I was transferred to a University College London hospital, and the lead paediatrician of the natal unit that came to speak to me looked out of sorts, but he had this air of calm. He was white, ginger-haired, with dreadlocks all the way down to his waist. I've never seen that before. He gave me all the statistics. He said, 'She's coming early, and we'll have to take her in because she'll need neo-natal care. The only thing she's got on her side is that she's got a good strong heart rate, which means that she's likely to be a girl. And her rate of survival is much higher than if she were a boy statistically speaking.' He said they're going to do everything to save the baby, etc. Now, I was set to lose everything; she had something like a two per cent survival rate and came out of the other end with more. Then the doctor said, 'Now I've given you the statistics. I want you to throw it out the window, and I'll tell you a little story. There's this gentleman that used to get onto a train and go to the same holiday destination, the same activities, every year. He used to love it, and he would come home feeling fantastic. One day he had to change trains, but he fell asleep and ended up in a different destination. He's out there lost and doesn't know what to do. He doesn't know how to get to the holiday place, but he knows how to get home. So, he thought I'm here now, let me make the most of it. And he had the most fantastic time; nothing like his usual holiday destination, but a fantastic time all the same. He didn't intend it or plan for it, but he ended up in a place where he made the most of it and went home with fantastic memories and experiences and another holiday destination.' The point of the paediatrician's story is that, despite what you think you know and despite whatever the odds are, it won't always be the case that what you set out to achieve will be done. But the journey in and of itself has an important purpose. You may not plan for something, but that does not mean that you cannot reap the rewards, benefits, and enjoyment from it. It's a matter of mindset. So go for it; you don't know what's on the other side. So it is for women of colour who are unwitting leaders to go for it; you owe it to yourself first and foremost. Besides, if you must know, women have been challenging the status quo for centuries and defying pre-existing odds.

What I ask of anybody, specifically of any woman of colour, is to give what you can, as much as you can, whether generously or reluctantly, because there will always be benefits from giving. When you put yourself out there, you help not only yourself, you help everybody, too. It's not a responsibility for you to do so, but there are far-reaching benefits. As women of colour, we have been patient long enough. We have contributed way too much with too little reward, and now it's our time to shine.

As for me, I'll continue being involved in this London Community Land Trust project for as long as possible. I want to see a viable plot of land for every generation come under community land trust management. The traditional patriarchal leaders have failed in their responsibilities catastrophically. I saw it happening in the housing association. So getting the opportunity to be involved with this CLT revealed the solution to a problem that local councils were contributing towards. We happen to be the largest in London, but I want to see other community land trust projects doing similar things to ours. Whilst social housing takes care of the most vulnerable, there are high-earning people who can afford housing. And then there are all those who fall in between. They aren't the most vulnerable, and they earn an average wage. I want to see those people, families, and young people out of university being given housing security. Once upon a time, you could leave university, get a job, buy a house. Young people can't do that anymore. The mental health problems that arise as a result of housing insecurity affect everybody. When you give stability and security to those groups, we all thrive successfully as a nation. I want to continue being a part of that: identifying this problem and getting secure homes for those people who are working hard to stay in London. The Windrush Generation came here and arguably had one of the biggest impacts in rebuilding Britain after the Second World War. Their children's children are now struggling to stay in Brixton, in Hackney, wherever it is. This is their home, and I want to help them remain there. One of our steering group members at the Youth Advocacy Academy said, 'I don't want to be travelling on a train for two hours just to visit my mom's grave in Brixton.'

'There I was telling my daughters there are no limits; there are no boundaries. Reach for whatever you want to reach for, yet the only female in their life was not presenting that to them. I thought, if I want them to go and take on the world, they have to see somebody take on the world. And that was it; I changed.'

— Razia

CHAPTER 11

Vanessa: The Independent Film Producer

In years gone by, women TV newsreaders were a rare breed. Having achieved the stuff of little girls' dreams, they were widely regarded as glamorous, exceptional beings who had dared to challenge the masculine face of national TV news. Such women tended to generate a buzz, a mixture of envy, curiosity and, of course, sexism!

My Page 1 Woman was one such trailblazer, appointed at a time when black news presenters were countable on three fingers. As a woman, she was greeted with the usual buzz. As a black woman, that buzz included a huge dollop of racist anger and abuse. And this was from folks who couldn't bear the sight of a smart black woman bucking the prevailing stereotypes presenting on their TV screens. This hatred and racist slur came not just from viewers but also from colleagues, too cowardly to disclose their names. And what was the broadcaster's response? Silence… until my Page 1 Woman demanded action.

It takes a special kind of woman to work in this kind of environment under this kind of pressure. But that's Vanessa Kirkpatrick for you, although she would never ever brand herself as 'special.' A woman of courage, determination, and tenacity; a woman with bags of resilience, a woman with a passion for social justice since she was a schoolgirl, a woman whose introversion belies her ability to challenge when racists rear their ugly heads. And challenge she did, throughout and beyond her time on-screen.

In those unenlightened days, long before 'unconscious bias,' George Floyd, and Black Lives Matter, Vanessa's support was restricted to the very few in her network with a keen grasp of the nature of racism. So her career pathway was one she walked in isolation, not quite knowing who she could trust for much of the time.

But how did this former school head girl and public speaking champ, who eschews the leader label for herself, make it in the media industry? How did she walk that lonely road in a white male-dominated profession and achieve success as a black woman? Here's Vanessa in her own words.

THE INTERVIEW

Claudia: What do you do for a living, Vanessa?

Vanessa: I'm an independent film producer. Prior to that, I was a development producer. I'm currently working on a documentary with an amazing director, Paul Sapin. It's his story about a miscarriage of justice in 1968 during the American Civil Rights movement. We are investigating the impact of this travesty of justice on what was once a thriving black community in the USA. So that's what I am doing at the moment.

My role as producer normally involves coming up with a story and then assembling a crew, including a director, to help bring it to the screen. This one is actually the director's story because of his personal connections to the events. I'm responsible for finding funding, arranging, hiring members of the creative team, and overseeing all of the other elements of production and post-production right up until release. It's for cinema release rather than television, which means that we can have greater control over the story. Because, quite often, you go to a television commissioner, and they love the idea, but then they want to change the storyline.

These types of documentaries take a long period of time. It can be extremely exhausting. You have to find all sorts of access to funding and backers. But then, when you realise that documentaries like this can be 10 years in the making, and you think, 'Hey, I've got time.' You just don't give up.

My career began in television as a consultant. I then went on to become a researcher, then a reporter, then a newsreader, and then producer/director, which I've now done for 18 years.

Little girls often dream about being on TV presenting the news. But I went on-screen because I thought I ought to, not because I wanted to. When I joined, I always wanted to be behind the scenes producing and directing. I thought there were stories that I could tell. But I didn't necessarily want to read or be seen reading the stories. And it was for the same reason that I came off the screen—because I didn't enjoy it. I felt very self-conscious. But also, I had some pretty unpleasant experiences while I was on-screen, which I may or may not have had, had my role been off-screen full-time.

In those days, your being on-screen involved multi-tasking. You had to have a wide variety of skills, and it's highly competitive. I felt that I had to demonstrate that I had other skills such as producing and directing. So that's one reason why I came off-screen in the end. A lot of colleagues couldn't believe it. They said, 'Why would you want to come off? You've got status. People recognise you. They want you to open garden fetes.' Well, being on-screen reading the news isn't as simple as it looks. If you're a very good newsreader, you'll make it look really easy. But there are all sorts of things going on in your earpiece. Four or five people are talking to you at the same time. Then you've got the background noise of the production. You've got people in front of you, you've got a crew, you have to concentrate on so many things and make it look seamless and relatively easy. And the better you are at it, the more you're criticised. 'Oh, she just reads autocue.' But it's not like that at all.

During my first week on air, I had a baptism of fire. My first two broadcasts were absolutely dreadful. During the first one, I was like an automaton. And the second one, the cue operator completely messed up and gave me the wrong running order. I started reading it, and I had people shouting in my ear, 'Vanessa, you're in item one. You should be in item seven; go to your hard copy.' Of course, because I was relying on the autocue, my sheets were all over the place. But the viewers couldn't see that because it was just basically a head and shoulder shot. So I was looking down, trying to find the right script to read from, and it seemed hours before I got to it. That baptism of fire taught me an important lesson: never rely on anybody else. Be prepared.

After leaving school, I graduated from Leeds University with a degree in politics. I went on to do various post-graduate works. My supervisor, an amazing woman, was writing a book on mul ticulturalism in education and literature. She asked me to work as her researcher. This actually put me in good stead for a career in TV, even though I wasn't sure of my career path at the time. Off the back of this work, just a couple of years later, I was invited to act as a consultant to a series being made by Yorkshire Television on multiculturalism in education. The series received a Times Education Award. In my other post-grad, the university hired me as a research assistant on a project it was developing with the Lucas Aerospace Shop Stewards Combine Committee. Faced with large-scale nationwide redundancies, the Lucas Plan advocated an alternative strategy, arguing that state support would be better put to developing products that society needed rather than the state supporting workers through paying redundancy money. The project was actually nominated for a Nobel Peace Prize.

Claudia: What was it about the media that appealed to you so much that you applied for those jobs rather than, for example, becoming a nurse?

Vanessa: I didn't go searching for those jobs. They just came along. I actually wanted to be a lawyer. I saw an advert in *The Guardian* newspaper for a television researcher with Granada Television. I really didn't think I had a shot at getting it, as Granada was one of the biggest broadcasters in television at the time. But I was encouraged, virtually coerced, into applying by my partner. He said, 'You've got credentials. You've got background and qualifications. Why aren't you looking at this job?' So I applied to get him off my back, to be honest. I sent in a straightforward factual CV with a covering note: 'I look forward to hearing from you.' As simple as that. I didn't sell myself, basically. I was absolutely shocked when I got called for an interview. I had to go through two interview panels before I recognised that I had to take this seriously and prepare myself. I realised that one of my strengths was the stories I could tell and the contacts I had that would be useful for Granada. And I thought, 'Yes, I can do this.' But I had no ambition beyond being a researcher. I could help feed stories to the newsroom and the documentary departments. And that's how short-sighted and limited my vision was.

I went for it because, first of all, I thought I had credentials that were absolutely appropriate. I liked telling stories, and I wanted to tell them in a particular way, from a particular perspective. I thought that there was a voice that was lacking. Now I know it was the black voice. But at the time, I wasn't really conscious of why I was attracted to that post.

There are two areas I've always been interested in: politics and the law. And I was thinking about the commonality between those two interests. It's something to do with people, social justice, exposing and rectifying wrongs, I think. My father was always talking about injustice at home. I remember going to the USA with my mum, aged 14, and an elderly homeless guy was begging me for money. I remember wondering about the injustice that could cause someone to beg from a 14-year-old. Well, I didn't go into either profession. And as I said before, this researcher job just came along—the story of my career, by the way; people are seeing something in me that I couldn't see myself and encouraging me to go for it.

So it just happened. But as soon as I got into that television newsroom and I was researching stories for other people to voice and present, I thought, 'Hang on a minute, that's not the way I researched it. You're leaving out some crucial things.' And I thought, 'I want to tell those stories.' That's why I thought I would go into producing and directing so that I could tell a more accurate version of the stories I'd researched.

Possibly the story that best exemplifies this is a documentary I made, 'I Didn't Know Black Men Could Fly', about a black pilot who fought in World War II. He had literally slipped below the radar. Living alone in the shadow of Battersea Power Station, he was still suffering the trauma of his experiences and battles 50 years on.

It was after I had left Granada for around 18 months that I was asked to return by Louise Nandy, the then Head of Regional News. They were considering me as a newsreader. I was shocked. It's relevant because it's what I was saying. I didn't seek the limelight. I was approached all the time. I never ever wanted to be in front of the camera because I was always uncomfortable there. I wanted to be behind it. But I needed to take advantage of those opportunities to show my diverse skills in order to improve my longevity.

When I was the researcher in Granada's newsroom, a colleague, Rachel, said several times, 'Vanessa, you would be really good on-screen. Why don't you do a screen test?' I refused. She then took me onto the roof of Granada Television, and I did several takes in front of the camera. She thought they were great. I said I'd take the tape to the editor, but I hid it in my drawer. Several weeks later, Rachel was rummaging through the drawer, and she found it and gave it to the news editor. I went on to become a reporter before I became a newsreader. How many times can you turn down an opportunity? It's ridiculous if you want career progression, and that's what they want you to do. What's the point of being there if you keep turning down opportunities? What is the point of denying that you may have other skills? Also, I grew into being an on-screen reporter and an on-screen newsreader. As much as I didn't like it, I was actually quite good at it.

Claudia: When you're being offered such great opportunities, what essential steps got you to where you are now?

Vanessa: There were awful racist things that happened at Granada that people don't know about, and I actually challenged them. That was an essential step because doing so boosted my confidence. I had to remember that my parents had had to go through far worse things. I knew I couldn't let them down. So I put on a face, even when I didn't feel like it. And that face became almost normal even though, deep down, I was scared. There's that analogy about you looking calm on the surface but, below the water, you're frantically paddling. It was like that.

But I'm a woman of colour with resilience in my DNA. We have that advantage from the moment we are born. We've got enormous strength. We should not be deterred. But it was tough. I had to choose which battles to fight because I couldn't fight them all every single day.

I had to surround myself with people I could trust, who shared my values—good colleagues and leaders who helped and supported me through bad times. I also associated myself with people who helped me take those important steps along the way. I've been very fortunate because it all helped to build my confidence when I suffered terribly from a lack of it.

Claudia: It seems as if this is a demanding public-facing profession. Tell us about the challenges you encountered on your career journey as a black woman, and how you overcame them?

Vanessa: It seemed clear from day one that my skin colour, and perhaps my gender, were problems for some people. At my first or second-morning news conference, the news editor wheeled her chair in a frenzy down to me and said, 'You do know, don't you, that you're only here because you're black?' And then wheeled her chair back. This was in my first two weeks of induction, so I knew things wouldn't be as happy as I expected. I tried to rationalise it, wondering whether she was trying to warn me of the obstacles and problems I might encounter. Or whether she was trying to undermine me. I decided on the latter. She was never particularly pleasant to me, but I knew where she was coming from. I didn't challenge that one, by the way, because that was far too early in my career at Granada.

It didn't particularly faze me because it wasn't the first time I'd come across that sort of attitude. But not long after, I was out on a shoot, and the crew were going absolutely crazy about immigration and saying all immigrants should be sent back to where they came from. One of the things you learn as a researcher is that you've got to look after your crew. That means ensuring they get a break for a one hour, three-course lunch with hot and cold options; otherwise, they claim a meal allowance, and you gain a reputation for being a poor catering manager! So I'm thinking, 'Okay, first of all, I've got a job to do: get it in the can, write a script, get it edited.' And I'm sitting here listening to my crew coming out with racist vitriol against a human rights issue and wondering whether I would get the shots I needed, given their clear antipathy to the item. And, at the same time, I'm thinking about where we can eat in two hours. I decided to let it ride. But as soon as I got back, I complained to the programme producer. She apparently looked into it and said that I didn't have to work with that crew again as if that somehow solved the problem. I'm not aware that she spoke to them. She didn't say whether they had been reprimanded. Certainly, nothing was conveyed to me.

The fact is I wasn't taken seriously. Similarly, a few years later, when it was announced internally that I was going to go on-air as a newsreader, 'Journ. Journ'—an internal portal for journalists to convey their concerns anonymously about various sorts of management policies—carried racial abuse that I was taking jobs from 'blonde, blue-eyed girls,' that I was only going on-air because I was black. So this was clearly coming from colleagues, people actually sitting opposite, working with me in the newsroom or elsewhere in the company. It was repetitive. I made a complaint to the editor. In a benign way, HE asked ME what I wanted HIM to do about it.

When I did go on-air, I got hate-mail, violent threats, that sort of thing, from viewers. But I didn't show them to anybody due to the reception I'd already received from my colleagues and the editor. I kept those letters and stupidly took them home where they contaminated my home space. One day, I decided to show one of the abusive letters to the programme editor. They called in the police. Interestingly, although the viewers' letters continued after that, the internal abuse stopped immediately.

But the abuse and those letters spurred me on. They made me determined to show how good I was. But, in showing how good you are, you make the job look easy. So, I was in a catch-22 situation, which I didn't know how to deal with. One day I said something to a friend who worked with me in the newsroom. To my extreme disappointment, she said, 'Vanessa, it's the same as somebody saying they don't like you because you've got ginger hair.' Clearly, she didn't get it.

At that point, I decided to reach out to another black newsreader from another channel. I told her about the hate mail, the violent threats, the racist stuff that I was getting. She shared similar experiences and sort of agreed for us to go public and talk about the racism and isolation that black people in the industry experienced. But did she ever get back to me? No. She didn't want to raise her head above the parapet. I was immensely disappointed.

But I used to get some really lovely letters, too, from viewers, although the horrid stuff was proportionally larger. They would say, 'You're our favourite news reader.' And there was one guy, a fashion designer, who said he wanted to make outfits for me, which was quite flattering. When you go on-screen or go public in your work, whether it's on television or in magazines, it's a vanity exercise, isn't it? You've got to present yourself in a particular way because the whole persona is part of what you're selling.

I've always been a very private person. So I cannot think of anything more contradictory than me being on-screen. I know a lot of people, black women in particular, who were jealous of me because they wanted that for themselves. When I was first on-screen, a black woman was standing in front of me in the queue in Kendals with her daughter. When I asked the assistant if they were being served, the black woman yelled at me, 'Do you think just because you're on television you're better?'

I was getting knocked from all sides. It felt very lonely. I wanted to find people who shared my values who would go along with me, but they were few and far between. And, sadly, my network of friends was a very small group of white women. I could count them on one hand. But they still didn't get how racism worked.

Claudia: How did you decide which of those incidents to challenge and which to leave alone?

Vanessa: It's about what you can prove. Because the problem with racism and sexism that you may face in any industry is identifying what is provable and how much energy you can put into demonstrating what is. That's why I have a problem with the phrase 'casual racism'. I don't think that there's any such thing as casual racism. But imagine if there was a production assistant who frequently referred to me as 'Sunshine' in a patronising way. The first time she used it, I was still a rookie. I didn't understand something that she had written on the production schedule. And I asked her about it, very politely, very calmly, quite deferentially actually. She didn't like it. She said, 'Listen, Sunshine, if you don't get it, I know what I'm doing.' She wouldn't have spoken to a white researcher like that. I didn't challenge her because I was very new to the job. So it's about deciding where you put your energy and where you think you can prove something. It's tough. Similarly, the incident with the news editor I referred to earlier; I've since wanted to talk to her about that.

Claudia: You've come a long way at a time when the media profession was relatively closed to people of colour. What was your greatest lightbulb moment that gave you a significant insight into your capabilities?

Vanessa: When I was 11 years old at the Wolverhampton Grammar Technical school. Mr. H, the music teacher, referred to some children waiting to come into the class with, 'Oh my God, look at these Pakis coming in.' I was absolutely horrified. I went to the deputy head, and I made a complaint that he had made a racist comment about these boys. At the end of the summer term assembly, it was announced that he wouldn't be returning. I remember smirking at this news. He was going to a school on the Isle of Wight, which I thought was so appropriate and so ironic. I thought, 'Gosh, I've got the power to make things happen.' That was my lightbulb moment.

That experience propelled me to always want to deal with situations. And I'm pretty proud of that moment because I took a risk. Mr. H knew that I had made a complaint about him. He asked me into the music room at the end of a class. I wasn't sure why, and I felt a sense of foreboding that something was going to happen. Anyway, he didn't mention the complaint; he just referred to me by my maiden name and said, 'You could go far in life, but I think you need to learn a little bit of humility.' I actually don't recall feeling nervous, anxious, or frightened by that.

Those little experiences embed themselves in your mind somewhere. You don't know when they're going to come into play. They've helped to build my resilience and determination. They have helped me make decisions about what I say when I say it, and what action I should take. It was a really important lightbulb moment.

Claudia: What one resource has been really crucial to your success?

Vanessa: It has to be my mother. I absolutely adored her, and still do. I wish I had appreciated just how funny, witty, intelligent she was at the time. And I occasionally go through letters that she sent me after I left home. They were just so brilliantly written, so poetic.

My mother travelled alone to England in around 1953, ahead of my father (who was working in the States at the time). She came on a plane ticket paid for by her mother, who had also found her a place to live before she moved into hospital accommodation while she trained as a nurse. I rather liked that my maternal grandmother—Miss Eugenie, who had an esteemed corner shop on the top of a hill in Oracabessa in St. Mary, Jamaica, wanted far better for her daughter. So she scrimped and saved for her. And so my mother left her hometown long before Enoch Powell's clarion call to people from the Caribbean to pretty much come and service the NHS.

I have pictures of my mother on her own, in a nurses' home, starting life by herself. She is standing beside a Rediffusion television. She carved an exceptional career in nursing. Some 15 years later, she became a Matron, Senior Nursing Officer, and to head the maternity wing of Walsall Manor Hospital, which was pretty spectacular for a black woman of her time.

My mother was my resource because she tried to give me confidence—self-belief. She would quite often get irritated that I didn't have self-belief. She had the most glorious spirit about her. And her smile! I'm looking at pictures of her right now. She was my role model, and I wanted to be like her because she worked so hard for her success. How could I not live up to what she achieved and what she went through all those years ago? It would be a shame to let down her legacy.

She set standards for me to strive for, although she was pretty tough. I can remember when I passed my 11plus, and I got my results through the letterbox. I ran upstairs, where she was on the landing ironing. I said, 'Mummy, I've passed.' She said, 'Okay, now you've just got to get your O levels and your A levels.' There wasn't any, 'Well done, darling.' It came later that day. And that's because she had to work so hard. 'Don't rest on your laurels' was pretty much what she was saying.

My lack of self belief was probably because I was brought up as an only child, as my sister, who was seven years older, was in Jamaica. I didn't really know her until I was about 12 when she came to the UK and lived with us until she left to pursue a career in nursing. I was shy and never had the confidence to socialise. I knew that I was a bright kid. In fact, I found that a little bit of a burden because my parents would say, 'Vanessa is the bright one.' I always felt that remark was extremely unfair to my sister.

I used to do things that I didn't really want to do to build my confidence. Things like being in school plays, being head girl (elected by my peers), and entering public speaking competitions. I won the Chamber of Commerce trophy for a speech on inequality and injustice, things I've always wanted to address.

Claudia: So being a leader came quite early in your life, Vanessa. So what does leadership mean to you?

Vanessa: Leadership is obviously about inspiring, motivating, and taking people along with you into unchartered territory. That's sort of an objective, neutral description of leadership which anybody would agree with. But we know that there are bad leaders, and there are good leaders. Good leaders lead by example and go where they're demanding that other people go with them.

Claudia: How has that informed your role as a black woman leader?

Vanessa: I don't think I am a leader, or if I am, it's unintended. And it's definitely with a lowercase 'L'. I don't think that I have the qualities of being a leader, and I've never asked anybody to follow me. As a film producer, I guess I'm a leader with a small 'L'. You have to keep people going because there are so many bumps in the road.

I may have done things that have inspired other people. For example, over the last couple of years, I've been asked to go into schools as a mentor, and I've talked to young girls, in particular, about how they can enter the media industry if that's what they want to do. I talk about the challenges that they might face and the positives because I've had some great times at Granada and in the media. So I give them, hopefully, some positive notes about making their way, whether in the media or any other industry. It's about being positive. It's about daring to take risks. It's about deciding which battles you're going to fight, because there will be battles. Life is exhausting enough as it is, particularly for young people who are going through all sorts of other things in their physical and mental development. And it is about finding people around you that will support your development. I don't know if that makes me a thought-leader. I've been asked to go in, but I just want to share my experiences and hopefully leave them with some optimism and determination. I do it because I've got something to share. I don't see myself as a leader, but I do have something to offer.

Claudia: So, although you see yourself as a leader with a small 'L', what would you say are your three top tips for women of colour who want to be leaders in their field?

Vanessa: As women of colour, resilience is in our DNA. That gives us an advantage. So don't be cowed when your opponents want to silence you because of your ideas and the colour of your skin. Stand up for yourself and what you believe in. You'll breathe fresh air. You'll know that you're fighting oppression. You have a responsibility to people who have gone before you and who went through far, far worse. You are carrying on a tradition of fighting and protesting against oppression. It's about maybe going on demonstrations or putting up two fingers at somebody, or whatever it is. It's about being a strong woman. I think that's just so important and so liberating. It's wonderful. It's like drinking a fresh glass of water, and when you do that, you feel great.

I've been writing about the stuff that I went through, particularly at Granada, and the fact that I didn't put up with a lot of their nonsense. So I can at least look back on it all with a very clear conscience. It feels good. And it's something that I passed on to my son. He is so incredibly proud of me. And as I'm getting older, I'm actually on a second wind. I'm speaking out more about this stuff; that's why I'm talking to young women who want to get into the industry because I'm saddened that things haven't really moved on as fast as they ought to have.

My second tip: lift as you climb. I can't remember who said it, but a good leader will create pathways for others to follow. It's wonderful and so satisfying to see other people thriving. And it is about creating that elevator so that women, particularly women of colour, are going to reach, and maybe go beyond their potential.

My third tip is to surround yourself with people who share the same values but who may also disagree with you. People you can have honest, open conversations with so that you can learn to develop your mind and your arguments. People who can also help you. But they have to be a positive influence. You have to be confident that you're covering each other's backs because, inevitably, there are going to be putdowns in public life, and you need to be there for each other. These people will share a common purpose with you—to create a better world.

You've got to just have people around you who you can disagree with because agreeing with each other 100 per cent is stultifying. You're never going to get anywhere if you only talk to people who agree with you 100 per cent. I love having a debate. That's one of the things I've enjoyed most about working on my current documentary film, for instance. And also, in my relationship with my partner, we have completely different points of views on things, but I don't mind that. I've developed him, and he's developed me, and it's fantastic. I find it so energising. A lot of my friends, although we come from a very similar radical point of view, also have differences of opinion to mine. That's wonderful. But the point is that we each have this sympathy and concern for other people. And that is what is really important.

Surround yourself with the right people, and they will be there for you when the going gets tough. And it will get tough if you're in public life. But even if you're not in public life, you'll still need the support of those people someday, somehow.

'I went for it because, first of all, I thought I had credentials that were absolutely appropriate. I liked telling stories, and I wanted to tell them in a particular way, from a particular perspective. I thought that there was a voice that was lacking. Now I know it was the black voice.'

— Vanessa

CHAPTER 12

Summary

"Take pride in knowing that your struggle will play the biggest role in your purpose."

—Melanie Maynard

Sometimes we need to remind ourselves that any life lived fully will have 'life contours'. There will be contradictions, complexities and trade-offs and the means by which these are ironed out. These small shifts are present in the lives of my 10 Page 1 Women, of course, but they are also intertwined in the journey of this book.

First, they are present in my own mixed and contradictory feelings of exasperation and pride. I feel exasperation that the marginalisation of women, and particularly black and Asian women, remains ever-present. Overcoming it still requires concerted active opposition from many more people. But, the pride I feel in these women, and that I could interview and then write about them making a difference in the world undeterred, far outshines my exasperation.

Second, they are present in the construction of the Success Equation. It became evident that every one of these women manifested determination, resilience, resistance and purpose. However, it was the individual interplay of these elements, in terms of sequence, strength and explicitness, that enabled their success. Two aspects, in particular, emerged in contradictory ways - purpose and success, neither of which were explicit at the start. 'Purpose' is a well-evidenced business and personal development requirement for any success; without it, drift and fatalism are likely to occur. However, for these women, purpose, once it emerged, anchored and shaped determination, resilience and resistance. When we add the additional, unrelenting colour-coded barriers they had to surmount, we end up with substantial women whose 'success' is more likely than not.

'Success' here is constructed by ignoring, bypassing, or perhaps opposing its conventional trappings of vast profits and fame, for example, and fuelling purpose in the service of others rather than for self. Again, these both emerged from contradictions and complexities. Indeed, promptings during their interviews had the effect of making these concepts more explicit.

Witness the riches that can accumulate from a fertile blending of clear purpose and the three other elements: Jax's thriving mental health charity; Razia's successful affordable housing campaign, and Marsha's flourishing young women's development charity. Add to these the additional common life events that triggered choices in how they responded: Netty's negotiation of personal tragedy, Sherry's opportunity awareness, Sharda's reshaping her early influences or Mandu's experience of and resistance to inequality.

Finally, to iron out some contradictions and complexities about the efficacy of my Success Equation, I asked myself, does it stand up to scrutiny? Is it necessary for success? Do successful black and Asian women become so because of it? Can other black and Asian women make use of it? To address such questions, bear in mind that the book is a retrospective template placed on lived experience. Nonetheless, from what I know as an experienced coach for women, I see that it stands up to scrutiny and answers those questions.

Yes, the success equation is necessary for success – although the elements may emerge in more disorganised ways than they appear here. Do successful black and Asian women become so because of it? Well, success is highly unlikely without it. The equation sustains them when life gets tough and keeps them pushing ahead. Again, the interplay and prioritising of the elements may vary, and the additional strengths of each individual will play a part. It is also worth noting that the Success Equation will be more productive where other aspects are in play, for example, having a growth mindset, effective business planning, strategic thinking, the need for more flexible responses when business as usual fails, and having goals rather than relying on habit orientation. Alongside all of that, rising to challenges and allowing oneself to be stretched and developed and making the most of new insights along the way helps too. When I think about the women interviewed in this book, I can see that their identity and related lived experiences are at the root of their Success Equation.

Can other black and Asian women make use of it, regardless of background, role or sector? Yes, and I would encourage them to individualise the Success Equation elements, adding their own unique energy, appetite and strengths. And if support is needed, coaching is an incredibly useful resource for developing these elements in a personalised way.

Finally, the limiting factors which attempt to disrupt black and Asian success stories will not voluntarily vanish. These women used their power to resist, to harness and shape their resistance. That's what makes them undeterred.

My hope for this book is that these ten women inspire other everyday women to identify their purpose and apply the equation in their own lives to become successful leaders too.

So, what have you learned from these Page 1 Women that you can apply on your journey? Go ahead and identify which of them you relate to most and learn from her because if she can do it, undeterred, so can you.

Claudia Crawley is an award-winning mentor, career coach and executive coach for women in social work-related professions. A former social work senior manager, Claudia founded Winning Pathways Coaching in 2010 to further her passion for equality and diversity and to support as many women as possible in their personal and professional lives. As an author and feminist, Claudia has written extensively about gender equality and women's development. In 2010, she coined the Page 1 Woman concept to showcase the achievements of ordinary women, which she shared on her website and across social media. Claudia has many years' experience of anti-racist action and in 2020 began developing race equality allies with the Women's Equality Party. Her mission is to change the world, one woman, at a time.

LIST OF ORGANISATIONS

Chapter 1:

Black Ballad: a UK based lifestyle digital magazine that shares life experiences from the perspective of black women. - https://blackballad.co.uk/

Chapter 3:

The Women's Equality Party: a new British political party that brings together all genders from diverse backgrounds and beliefs, in pursuit of gender equality. https://www.womensequality.org.uk/

London School of Economics & Political Science (LSE) – a British Russell Group university which specialises in social sciences. https://www.lse.ac.uk/

Eton College: an English public school for boys, founded in 1440 by Henry V1, and based in Eton in Berkshire. Well known for its wealth, history and distinguished alumni. https://www.etoncollege.com/

The Burlington Club: a space that brings together Chefs from Michelin star restaurants and a collection of the finest bartenders in the West-End of London.

City Hall: HQ of the Greater London Authority, ie. The mayor of London and the London Assembly. https://www.london.gov.uk/about-us/our-building-and-squares/how-find-city-hall

Chapter 4:

Tesco: a British multi-national supermarket for groceries and other general goods, and the third largest retailer globally measured by gross revenues and the ninth largest globally measured by revenues.

The World Transformation Organisation: an organisation that campaigns to unite thousands of change-makers to inspire and touch 1 million

lives on World Transformation Day. https://www.sonyamortonfirth.com/
kalpesh-patel-impacting-the-world-transforming-it-every-day/

Landmark Worldwide: a company, headquartered in San Francisco, which offers personal and professional development programmes worldwide. Focus is on people achieving success, satisfaction and greatness. https://www.landmarkworldwide.com/

Andy Harrington's Power to Achieve: a 3 day experience designed to optimise individuals' potential. https://www.powertoachieve.co.uk/optin-36315013

Chapter 5:

Julian Campbell Foundation: a charity established to help children, teenagers and young adults who have undiagnosed mental health issues. https://juliancampbellfoundation.org/

Chapter 6:

Breakfree Forever Consultancy Ltd: an organisation that helps entrepreneurs and small business owners to write their book, gain visibility and position themselves as an authority in their field. https://breakfreeforever-consultancyltd.vipmembervault.com/

The Coaching Academy: a British company that offers professional training in the practical skills of coaching. https://www.the-coaching-academy.com/

Andy Harrington's Professional Speakers Academy: a comprehensive training programme and membership for business owners and leaders who want to be confident public speakers and use this skill to develop their business. https://www.andyharrington.com/psa

Chapter 7:

National Society for the Prevention of Cruelty to Children (NSPCC): a leading UK children's charity that specialises in child protection and has statutory powers to safeguard children at risk of abuse. https://www.nspcc.org.uk/

Children And Family Court Advisory And Support Service (Cafcass): a non-departmental public body established to safeguard and promote the welfare of children going through the family justice system due to parental separation or divorce, care proceedings; or adoption. https://www.cafcass.gov.uk/